Sixth Workshop on Universal Dependencies (UDW 2023)

Washington, DC, USA
9-12 March 2023

ISBN: 978-1-7138-9065-2

Printed from e-media with permission by:

Curran Associates, Inc.
57 Morehouse Lane
Red Hook, NY 12571

CURRAN ASSOCIATES INC.
proceedings
.com

Some format issues inherent in the e-media version may also appear in this print version.

Association for Computational Linguistics
209 N. Eighth Street
Stroudsburg, Pennsylvania 18360

Phone: 1-570-476-8006
Fax: 1-570-476-0860

acl@aclweb.org

Additional copies of this publication are available from:

Curran Associates, Inc.
57 Morehouse Lane
Red Hook, NY 12571 USA
Phone: 845-758-0400
Fax: 845-758-2633
Email: curran@proceedings.com
Web: www.proceedings.com

UDW 2023

The Sixth Workshop on Universal Dependencies (UDW, GURT/SyntaxFest 2023)

Proceedings of the Conference

March 9-12, 2023

The UDW organizers gratefully acknowledge the support from the following sponsors.

The Georgetown College of Arts & Sciences, the Georgetown Faculty of Languages and Linguistics, and the Georgetown Department of Linguistics

GURT 2023
SYNTAXFEST
Washington, D.C.

1789
GEORGETOWN UNIVERSITY

Order copies of this and other ACL proceedings from:

Association for Computational Linguistics (ACL)
209 N. Eighth Street
Stroudsburg, PA 18360
USA
Tel: +1-570-476-8006
Fax: +1-570-476-0860
acl@aclweb.org

Introduction

Universal Dependencies (UD) is a framework for cross-linguistically consistent treebank annotation that has so far been applied to over 100 languages and aiming to capture similarities as well as idiosyncrasies among typologically different languages but also to facilitate multilingual natural language processing and enable comparative linguistic studies. The goal of the UD workshop is to bring together researchers working on UD, to reflect on the theory and practice of UD, its use in research and development, and its future goals and challenges. The Sixth Workshop on Universal Dependencies (UDW 2023) is for the first time part of GURT 2023, an annual linguistics conference held at Georgetown University which this year co-locates four related but independent events:

- The Seventh International Conference on Dependency Linguistics (Depling 2023)
- The 21st International Workshop on Treebanks and Linguistic Theories (TLT 2023)
- The Sixth Workshop on Universal Dependencies (UDW 2023)
- The First International Workshop on Construction Grammars and NLP (CxGs+NLP 2023)

The Georgetown University Round Table on Linguistics (GURT) is a peer-reviewed annual linguistics conference held continuously since 1949 at Georgetown University in Washington DC, with topics and co-located events varying from year to year.
In 2023, under an overarching theme of 'Computational and Corpus Linguistics', GURT/SyntaxFest continues the tradition of SyntaxFest 2019 and SyntaxFest 2021/22 in bringing together multiple events that share a common interest in using corpora and treebanks for empirically validating syntactic theories, studying syntax from quantitative and theoretical points of view, and for training machine learning models for natural language processing. Much of this research is increasingly multilingual and cross-lingual and requires continued systematic analysis from various theoretical, applied, and practical perspectives. New this year, the CxGs+NLP workshop brings a usage-based perspective on how form and meaning interact in language.
For these reasons and encouraged by the success of the previous editions of SyntaxFest, we —the chairs of the four events— decided to facilitate another co-located event at GURT 2023 in Washington DC.
As in past co-located events involving several of the workshops, we organized a single reviewing process, with identical paper formats for all four events. Authors could indicate (multiple) venue preferences, but the ultimate assignment of papers to events for accepted papers was made by the program chairs.
33 long papers were submitted, 11 to Depling, 16 to TLT, 10 to UDW and 10 to CxGs+NLP. The program chairs accepted 27 (82%) and assigned 7 to Depling, 6 to TLT, 5 to UDW and 9 to CxGs+NLP.
16 short papers were submitted, 6 of which to Depling, 6 to TLT, 10 to UDW and 2 to CxGs+NLP. The program chairs accepted 9 (56%) and assigned 2 to Depling, 2 to TLT, 3 to UDW, and 2 to CxGs+NLP.
Our sincere thanks go to everyone who is making this event possible: everybody who submitted their papers; Georgetown University Linguistics Department students and staff—including Lauren Levine, Jessica Lin, Ke Lin, Mei-Ling Klein, and Conor Sinclair—for their organizational assistance; and of course, the reviewers for their time and their valuable comments and suggestions. Special thanks are due to Georgetown University, and specifically to the Georgetown College of Arts & Sciences and the Faculty of Languages and Linguistics for supporting the conference with generous funding. Finally, we would also like to thank ACL SIGPARSE for its endorsement and the ACL Anthology for publishing the proceedings.
Owen Rambow, François Lareau (Depling2023 Chairs)
Daniel Dakota, Kilian Evang, Sandra Kübler, Lori Levin (TLT2023 Chairs)
Loïc Grobol, Francis Tyers (UDW2023 chairs)
Claire Bonial Harish Tayyar Madabushi (CxG+NLP2023 Chairs)
Nathan Schneider, Amir Zeldes (GURT2023 Organizers)
March 2023

Organizing Committee

Depling2023 Chairs

Owen Rambow, Stony Brook University
François Lareau, Université de Montréal

TLT2023 Chairs

Daniel Dakota, Indiana University
Kilian Evang, Heinrich Heine University Düsseldorf
Sandra Kübler, Indiana University
Lori Levin, Carnegie Mellon University

UDW2023 Chairs

Loïc Grobol, Université Paris Nanterre
Francis Tyers, Indiana University

CxGs+NLP2023 Chairs

Claire Bonial, U.S. Army Research Lab
Harish Tayyar Madabushi, The University of Bath

GURT2023 Organizers

Amir Zeldes, Georgetown University
Nathan Schneider, Georgetown University

GURT2023 Student Assistants

Lauren Levine, Georgetown University
Ke Lin, Georgetown University
Jessica Lin, Georgetown University

Program Committee

Program Committee for the Whole of GURT2023

Lasha Abzianidze, Utrecht University
Patricia Amaral, Indiana University
Valerio Basile, University of Turin
Emily Bender, University of Washington
Bernd Bohnet, Google
Claire Bonial, Army Research Lab
Gosse Bouma, University of Groningen
Miriam Butt, Universität Konstanz
Marie Candito, Université de Paris
Giuseppe G. A. Celano, Universität Leipzig
Xinying Chen, Xi'an Jiaotong University
Silvie Cinkova, Charles University Prague
Cagri Coltekin, Universität Tübingen
Stefania Degaetano-Ortlieb, Universität des Saarlandes
Éric Villemonte de la Clergerie, INRIA
Miryam de Lhoneux, KU Leuven
Valeria de Paiva, Topos Institute
Lucia Donatelli, Saarland University
Timothy Dozat, Google
Kim Gerdes, Université Paris-Saclay
Koldo Gojenola, University of the Basque Country
Loïc Grobol, Université Paris Nanterre
Bruno Guillaume, INRIA
Dag Trygve Truslew Haug, University of Oslo
Jena Hwang, Allen Institute for Artificial Intelligence
András Imrényi, Eötvös Lorand University
Alessandro Lenci, University of Pisa
Lori Levin, Carnegie Mellon University
Markéta Lopatková, Charles University Prague
Sylvain Kahane, Université Paris Nanterre
Jordan Kodner, State University of New York, Stony Brook
Sandra Kübler, Indiana University
Jan Macutek, Mathematical Institute, Slovak Academy of Sciences
Harish Tayyar Madabushi, University of Sheffield
Nicolas Mazziotta, Université de Liège
Alexander Mehler, Johann Wolfgang Goethe Universität Frankfurt am Main
Simon Mille, Dublin City University
Pierre André Ménard, Computer research institute of Montréal
Yusuke Miyao, The University of Tokyo
Simonetta Montemagni, ILC-CNR
Alexis Nasr, Aix Marseille Univ
Joakim Nivre, Uppsala University
Pierre Nugues, Lund University
Timothy John Osborne, Zhejiang University
Petya Osenova, Bulgarian Academy of Sciences
Robert Östling, Stockholm University

Simon Petitjean, Heinrich-Heine Universität Düsseldorf
Dirk Pijpops, Université de Liège
Michael Regan, University of Colorado, Boulder
Mathilde Regnault, Universität Stuttgart
Laurence Romain, University of Birmingham
Rudolf Rosa, Charles University Prague
Haruko Sanada, Rissho University
Beatrice Santorini, University of Pennsylvania
Giorgio Satta, Università degli studi di Padova
Sebastian Schuster, Universität des Saarlandes
Olga Scrivner, Rose-Hulman Institute of Technology
Ashwini Vaidya, Indian Institute of Technology, Delhi
Remi van Trijp, Sony Computer Sciences Laboratories Paris
Giulia Venturi, Institute for Computational Linguistics "A. Zampolli" (ILC-CNR)
Nianwen Xue, Brandeis University
Eva Zehentner, University of Zurich
Amir Zeldes, Georgetown University
Daniel Zeman, Charles University Prague
Heike Zinsmeister, Universität Hamburg
Hongxin Zhang, Zhejiang University

Table of Contents

Building a Universal Dependencies Treebank for a Polysynthetic Language: the Case of Abaza

Alexey Koshevoy[1, 2, *], Anastasia Panova[3], and Ilya Makarchuk[4]

[1]Laboratoire de Psychologie Cognitive, Aix-Marseille University, CNRS, Marseille, France
[2]Institut Jean Nicod, Département d'études cognitives, ENS, EHESS, CNRS, PSL University, Paris, France
[3]Department of Linguistics, Stockholm University, Stockholm, Sweden
[4]Linguistic Convergence Laboratory, HSE University, Russian Federation
[*]Corresponding author: alexey.koshevoy@univ-amu.fr

Abstract

In this paper, we discuss the challenges that we faced during the construction of a Universal Dependencies treebank for Abaza, a polysynthetic Northwest Caucasian language. We propose an alternative to the morpheme-level annotation of polysynthetic languages introduced in Park et al. (2021). Our approach aims at reducing the number of morphological features, yet providing all the necessary information for the comprehensive representation of all the syntactic relations. Besides, we suggest to add one language-specific relation needed for annotating repetitions in spoken texts and present several solutions that aim at increasing cross-linguistic comparability of our data.

1 Introduction

The Universal Dependencies (UD) framework (de Marneffe et al., 2021) provides a cross-linguistically universal annotation scheme, which, when necessary, allows language-specific extensions. The need for language-specific extensions becomes particularly evident when building a treebank for languages with polysynthetic morphology (on the features commonly considered polysynthetic, see, e.g., Mattissen (2017, p. 71-73)). For example, to account for nominal incorporation in Chukchi, Tyers and Mishchenkova (2020) introduce additional nodes for incorporated arguments of predicates.[1] In the treebank of St. Lawrence Island Yupik, Park et al. (2021) treat each morpheme as a token which requires seven additional dependency relations under the unspecified `dep` relation (`dep:infl`, `dep:aux`, etc.). In both cases the authors strive to create a more comprehensive representation of a polysynthetic language in UD, but the resulting annotation is not consistent with some of the UD principles. The UD approach assumes that the basic units are words (de Marneffe et al., 2021, p. 259), therefore, to achieve greater consistency, even in polysynthetic languages the word-based analysis should be favored over the morpheme-based analysis. In addition, we believe that such radical adjustments to UD as proposed for Yupik (Park et al., 2021) may be justified for one specific language (or one specific family) but generalization of this approach to all polysynthetic languages can be avoided. In this paper, we introduce a new way of dealing with polysynthetic morphology in UD and show that our approach aligns well with the UD framework. Specifically, we discuss the annotation of the treebank of Abaza, a polysynthetic Northwest Caucasian language.

2 Abaza

Abaza (ábaza bəzŝá, ISO 639-3: `abq`) is a polysynthetic language belonging to the Northwest-Caucasian family. According to the 2010 Russian census, it is spoken by approximately 38.000 speakers in the Karachay-Cherkes Republic, Russia. Additionally, Chirikba (2012) estimates that there are approximately 10.000 speakers of Abaza in Turkey. Abaza has two distinct variants — Tapanta and Ashkharywa. The data introduced in this paper comes from the Tapanta variant. Abaza has a rich written tradition, which has developped during the Soviet period. Abaza has a writing system that consists of a modified Cyrillic alphabet with the addition of one grapheme (I, "palochka"), which is used to indicate ejective consonants.

The polysynthetic nature of Abaza manifests itself mostly in verbal morphology. Abaza has a rich system of prefixes that are used for cross-referencing up to four verbal arguments. These prefixes indicate the number, person, gender, and grammatical role of each argument. As shown in Table 1, the personal prefixes form two distinct series – absolutive and oblique (including both ergative and indirect object markers). If the hearer

[1]See the same solution for Nahuatl in Pugh et al. (2022, p. 5018).

Proceedings of the Sixth Workshop on Universal Dependencies (UDW, GURT/SyntaxFest 2023), pages 1 - 6
March 9-12, 2023 ©2023 Association for Computational Linguistics

can recover the subject, object, and indirect object from context, they don not need to be overtly expressed by independent nominals.

	absolutive	oblique		absolutive	oblique
1sg	s(ə)-/z-		1pl	h(ə)-/ʕ-	
2sg.M	w(ə)-		2pl	ŝ(ə)-/ẑ-	
2sg.F	b(ə)-/p-		3pl	j(ə)-/∅	r(ə)-/d(ə)-
3sg.M	d(ə)-	j(ə)-	Rel	j(ə)-	z(ə)-
3sg.F		l(ə)-			
3sg.N	j(ə)-/∅-	a-/na-			

Table 1: The system of verbal cross-referencing prefixes (adapted from Arkadiev (to appear)).

In addition to cross-referencing prefixes, there are more than a dozen types of affixes that can be attached to the verbal form. These include temporal markers, voice markers, markers of negation, locative affixes, etc. The ordering of those affixes is shown in Table 2.

Although the basic word order is SOV, some variation is allowed. For instance, there are cases of arguments appearing in the postverbal position. In example (1), the absolutive subject *a-waʕá* (def-people) occurs in the rightmost position in the clause.[2]

(1) abar-awəj a-pš-ta
EMP-DIST 3SG.N.IO-similar-ADV
j-bzaza-kʷa-d a-waʕa
3PL.ABS-live-PL-DCL DEF-people
'Thus lived the people.'

3 Spoken corpus of Abaza

The treebank presented in this paper is based on data from the Spoken Corpus of Abaza.[3] This corpus was built using the `tsacorpus` platform (see Arkhangelskiy (2020) for a brief description of the platform). It contains 25 spoken texts recorded from 8 different speakers. The recordings were made in the village of Inžič-Čukun in the Karachay-Cherkess Republic, Russia, between 2017 and 2019. The total duration of recorded data is approximately one hour.

The texts contained in the Spoken Corpus of Abaza were initially transcribed using the Abaza orthography. Further, these transcriptions were converted into an IPA-based transcription. The participants of the Abaza research group provided interlinear glosses for each text based on the translations obtained from the speakers of Abaza. The texts were annotated using the ELAN software (Wittenburg et al., 2006), therefore each sentences is aligned with a corresponding audio segment.

4 Preprocessing

We devised a specific pipeline to convert ELAN files into ten-column CoNLL-U format. We started by extracting the glossing abbreviations from the interlinear annotations. As the corpus uses an idiosyncratic notation for glosses, we have created a mapping between the interlinear glosses from the corpus and the corresponding morphological features compatible with the CoNLL-U format. We then used the script[4] written by Francis Tyers to convert the cleaned sets of Abaza morphological features into UD morphological features using our mapping. The untransformed glosses were also preserved to be included in the MISC section of the CoNLL-U format. As the final step, we manually added lemmas to each wordform in the CoNLL-U annotations.

We choose to use the original Cyrillic-based orthography instead of the phonological transcription in our treebank for the following reason. The Abaza orthography is used in non-annotated texts available online: newspapers and works of fiction. Since we plan to train an automatic parsing model to annotate more data for this treebank, the model needs to be trained on the data which has the same orthography as in the texts that it will be used to annotate.

5 Morphology

Many of the categories expressed by affixes in Abaza cannot be easily converted to UD annotation. First, verbal forms often have locative prefixes, which specify the meaning of the root. For example, in (2) the verbal root on its own means 'to fly', but with the addition of the locative prefix *tə-* 'out', its meaning changes to 'fly away.'

(2) a-warba a-ʕʷara j-tə-pssʕa-ṭ
DEF-eagle DEF-nest 3SG.N.ABS-loc:out-fly-DCL
'The eagle flew out of its nest.' (Klyčev, 1994, p. 140)

Second, Abaza verbs can be modified by so-called event operators, which express aspectual meanings or modify the Aktionsart (lexical aspect) of the predicate, cf. two repetitive markers in (3).

[2]The list of abbreviations for glosses is provided in the Appendix.

[3]`http://lingconlab.ru/spoken_abaza/`

[4]`https://github.com/ftyers/ud-scripts/blob/master/conllu-feats.py`

-12	-11	-10	-9	-8	-7	-6	-5	-4	-3	-2	-1	0	+1	+2	+3	+4	+5	+6	+7
absolutive	subordination, negation	repetitive	potential, involuntative	applicatives	directional preverbs	locative preverbs	indirect object	ergative	negation	causative	sociative	root	directional suffixes	event operators	plural	aspect, tense	negation	past tense, modality	subordinators, force, emphasis

Table 2: The Abaza verbal template (adapted from Arkadiev (to appear)).

(3) h-ata-də-r-ca-χ-wa-n
1PL.ABS-rep-3PL.ERG-CAUS-go-re-IPF-PST
'they would again turn us [back]'

There is more than a hundred of different locative preverbs and more than fifteen event operators in Abaza (Klyčev, 1994; Tabulova, 1976, p. 204-215), so it is impossible to encode all these morphemes in an exhaustive set of UD morphological features. In addition, more than one locative preverb or event operator can occur in a wordform, therefore each of those affixes would require a separate feature. Finally, many locative prefixes and event operators are fully productive, so they cannot be easily attributed to derivation and thus ignored.

One way of dealing with this kind of morphology consists in treating all affixes as independent lexical items, as was suggested for St. Lawrence Island Yupik (Park et al., 2021), but this goes against the lexicalist approach adopted in the UD framework. Here we want to propose an alternative solution for the Abaza treebank. We suggest to keep the information about the meaning of each morpheme in the MISC section of CoNLL-U format. That way, it can still be available to the researchers that want to examine our data. At the same time, in the FEAT section we retain only those morphological features that are relevant to syntactic structure. Specifically, we decided to limit the grammatical features of Abaza encoded in UD to argument cross-referencing, valency-changing operations (reflexive, causative), finiteness, tense, mood, interrogativity and polarity. For example, compare the sentence (4) and its annotation in CoNLL-U format in Figure 1.

(4) s-pa a-q̇arč'a-kʷa
1SG.PR-son DEF-Karachai-PL
də-r-š'ə-n
3SG.H.ABS-3PL.ERG-kill-PST
d-sə-z-ʕa-r-g-χ-ṭ
3SG.H.ABS-1SG.IO-BEN-CSL-3PL.ERG-carry-RE-DCL
'the Karachays killed my son and brought [him to me]'

Example (4) contains two verbal forms — *də-r-š'ə-n* 'they killed him' and *d-sə-z-ʕa-r-g-χ-ṭ* 'they brought him to me'. Both verbs have cross-referencing markers which allow to identify syntactic relations between the predicates and their arguments. Final suffixes on verbal forms cumulatively express tense, mood and finiteness, and they are crucial for understanding the syntactic status of the predicate in the clause. The rest of the information present in the glosses of verbal forms — the cislocative prefix and the repetitive suffix — is not included in the FEAT section of the annotation because it is not relevant to syntax.

6 Syntax

In this paper, we propose to constrain the morphosyntactic information to the level of the morphological annotation so that the syntactic annotation does not differ from other languages present in UD. Overall, we were only required to add one language-specific relation (`dep:repeat`) and resolve minor complications with several expressions.

6.1 Repetitions

The data used in the Abaza treebank comes from spoken language and hence displays features that are not present in the written texts. In particular, our data contain multiple cases of word repetition, cf. the verb 'make' in (5).

(5) j-s-č'pa-l-əj-ṭ
3SG.N.ABS-1SG.ERG-make-HAB-PRS-DCL
awə-g'əj pirog-g'əj s-č'p-əj-ṭ <...>
DIST-ADD pie-ADD 1SG.ERG-make-PRS-DCL
'I make pies, I make...'

```
# sent_id = 57
# text_name = 0_muzhe_SanashokovaCKh_13072017_checked.eaf
# text = спа акъарчаква дырщын дсызгIаргхтI
# text_orth = с-па а-къарча-ква ды-р-щы-н д-сы-з-гIа-р-г-х-тI
# text_transcription = s-pa a-q̇arč'a-kʷa də-r-š'ə-n d-sə-z-ʕa-r-g-χ-ṭ
# text_rus = Сына убили карачаевцы и привезли.
1 спа па NOUN _ Number[psor]=Sing|Person[psor]=1 3 obj _ Gloss=1sg.pr-сын
2 акъарчаква къарча NOUN _ Definite=Def|Number=Plur 3 nsubj _
Gloss=def-карачаевец-pl
3 дырщын щра VERB _ Gender[abs]=Com|Number[abs]=Sing|Number[erg]=Plur|Person[abs]=3|
Person[erg]=3|Tense=Past|VerbForm=Fin 0 root _ Gloss=3sg.h.abs-3pl.erg-убить-pst
4 дсызгIаргхтI гара VERB _ Gender[abs]=Com|Number[abs]=Sing|Number[erg]=Plur|
Number[io]=Sing|Person[abs]=3|Person[erg]=3|Person[io]=1|Tense=Aor|VerbForm=Fin
3 conj _ Gloss=3sg.h.abs-1sg.io-ben-csl-3pl.erg-нести-re-dcl
```

Figure 1: An annotation fragment.

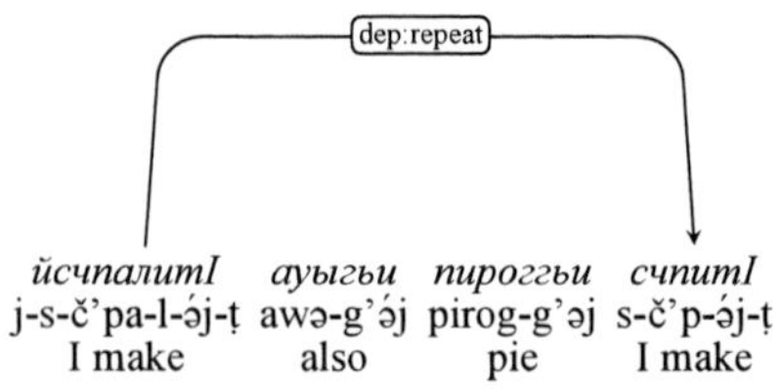

This phenomenon does not result from applying a grammatical rule (cf. reduplication expressing plurality or emphasis), and it does not fit into the existing set of UD syntactic relations. There is no speech repair, since the correct version of the word has already been uttered, so the `reparandum` relation cannot be employed in such cases. One might propose to use the `dislocated` relation but this relation is usually used for noun phrases that are fronted or postposed for reasons related to information structure (e.g., topicalization). However, what we are dealing with here is a result of hesitation about the next word, and the reason for repetition seems to be the intention of the speaker to fill the pause. Thus, we decided to introduce a new dependency relation `dep:repeat`, which encodes non-grammatical, non-repair repetitions.

6.2 Demonstratives

Demonstratives in Abaza can be used both as determiners (6) and as third person pronouns (7). A similar pattern is observed in many other languages of the world (Bhat, 2013), such as Buryat, Hindi or Aleut. According to the current UD guidelines, the POS tag constrains the set of possible dependency relations. For instance, the dependent of an `advmod`-relation can only be an adverb (`ADV`). Likewise, in (6) we had to tag the demonstrative as a determiner (`DET`) so it can be a dependent of a `det`-relation. By contrast, in (7) we had to tag the same demonstative as a pronoun (`PRON`) so it can be an object of the verb. A similar solution was proposed for Punjabi in Arora (2022, p. 5706).

(6) awat j-ʕa-n-χa-z
dist.pl REL.ABS-CSL-LOC-stay-PST.NFIN
a-wʕa-kʷa <...>
DEF-people-PL
'Those people who stayed <...>'

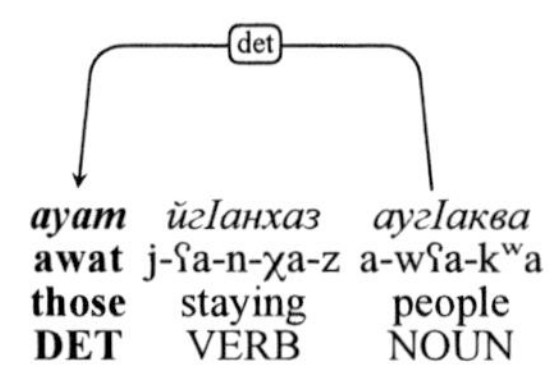

(7) awat s-č'pa-wa-mca
dist.pl 1SG.ERG-make-IPF-CVB
č-a-s-rə-š'ca-n <...>
RFL.ABS-3SG.N.IO-1SG.ERG-CAUS-get.used.to-PST
'I got used to making **them** <...>'

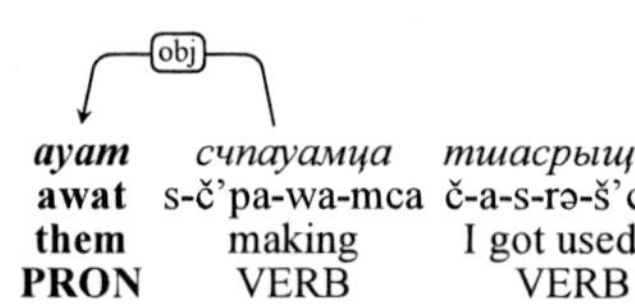

6.3 The word *asqan* 'time'

The morphosyntactic status of the word *asqan* 'time' is not always clear. Usually, it heads nominal phrases denoting time periods (8) ('in the time of the year 1929') and subordinate temporal clauses (9)('in the time when she came back').[5] Apparently, from the diachronic syntax perspective, in (8) *asqan* is a head of a noun phrase ('the time of the year'), and in (9) it is a head of a relative clause ('the time during which she came back'). However, we decided to simplify the annotation

[5]Temporal clauses in Abaza represent a subtype of relative clauses. The predicate of the temporal clause is marked with the special prefix *an-* rel.tmp.

of *asqan* in our treebank for two reasons. First, *asqan* in these contexts may be seen as an already grammaticalized element and thus requiring a different analysis. Second, if we adhere to the diachronic analysis, a user who would like to find examples with adverbials and adverbial clauses in Abaza would miss those with *asqan*. Nominal phrases with *asqan* are functionally equivalent to English adpositional phrases with 'in' or 'during', and relative clauses with *asqan* are functionally equivalent to English *when*-clauses. That is why we decided to annotate Abaza *asqan*-constructions similarly to their English counterparts. Thus, in the current version of the Abaza treebank *asqan* introducing temporal nominals is analyzed as a postposition, and *asqan* introducing temporal clauses is analyzed as a subordinating conjunction.

(8) awəj a-skʷšə zk'-əj
DIST.SG DEF-year thousand-COORD
ẑ-ŝ-əj ʕʷaẑə ẑ-ba asqan
nine-hundred-COORD twenty nine-CL.N time
d-ʕa-d-rə-j-d
3SG.H.ABS-CSL-3PL.ERG-CAUS-be_born-DCL
'She was born **in** 1929.'

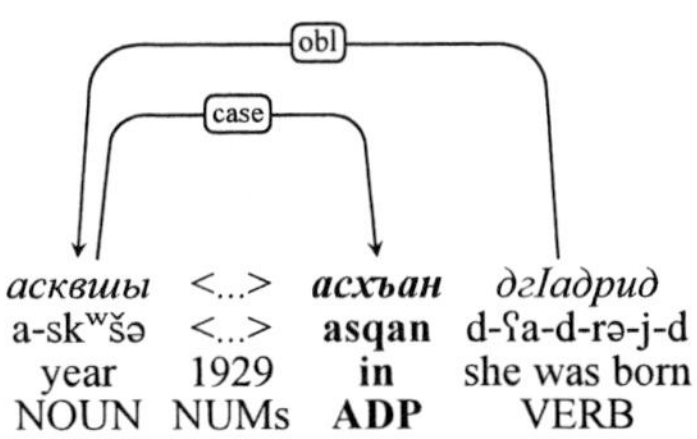

(9) <...> d-an-ʕa-j-χ asqan
3SG.H.ABS-REL.TMP-CSL-come-RE time
a-sabəj
DEF-child
d-g'-lə-m-dər-χ-d <...>
3SG.H.ABS-NEG.EMP-3SG.F.ERG-NEG-know-RE-DCL
'**When** she came back, she didn't know about the child <...>'

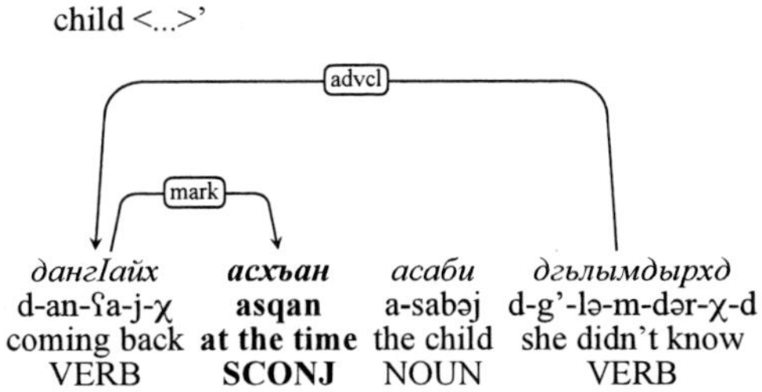

7 Conclusions

The Abaza treebank presented in this paper is the first case of a Northwest Caucasian language being added to UD. Abaza is a polysynthetic language, and thus it could be annotated on the level of individual morphemes, as suggested in (Park et al., 2021) for St. Lawrence Island Yupik. In this paper, we proposed a different approach which aims to minimize the morphological encoding, yet providing all necessary information for the analysis of syntactic relations. We showed that with the reduction of the number of the morphological features and some minimal adjustments to the set of dependency relations Abaza can be successfully annotated in the UD framework. Finally, we presented several solutions that aim at increasing the cross-linguistic comparability of our data.

Acknowledgements

This work is an output of a research project implemented as part of the Basic Research Program at the National Research University Higher School of Economics (HSE University). We thank Peter Arkadiev for his help, as well as other members of the "Aspects of Abaza Grammar" research group. We also thank Thierry Poibeau and Niko Partanen for their extensive help during the initial stage of this project. And, finally, we want to thank the anonymous reviewers for their very helpful comments.

References

Peter M. Arkadiev. to appear. Abaza. In Yury Koryakov, Yury Lander, and Timur Maisak, editors, *The Caucasian Languages. An International Handbook*. De Gruyter Mouton, Berlin.

Timofey Arkhangelskiy. 2020. Web Corpora of Volga-Kama Uralic Languages. *Finno-Ugric Languages and Linguistics*, 9(1-2).

Aryaman Arora. 2022. Universal Dependencies for Punjabi. In *Proceedings of the Thirteenth Language Resources and Evaluation Conference*, pages 5705–5711, Marseille, France. European Language Resources Association.

D. N. Shankara Bhat. 2013. Third person pronouns and demonstratives. In Matthew S. Dryer and Martin Haspelmath, editors, *The World Atlas of Language Structures Online*. Max Planck Institute for Evolutionary Anthropology, Leipzig.

Vyacheslav A. Chirikba. 2012. Rasselenie abxazov i abazin v Turcii [Survey of the Abkhazians and Abazas in Turkey]. *Džigetskij sbornik. vyp. 1. Voprosy ètno-kul'turnoj istorii Zapadnoj Abxazii ili Džigetii [The Jiget collection. I. Studies in the ethnic and cultural history of Western Abkhazia or Jigetia]*, (1):21–95.

Marie-Catherine de Marneffe, Christopher D. Manning, Joakim Nivre, and Daniel Zeman. 2021. Universal Dependencies. *Computational Linguistics*, 47(2):255–308.

Rauf N. Klyčev. 1994. *Lokal□no-preverbnoe obrazovanie glagolov abazinskogo jazyka [The locative preverbial derivation of verbs in Abaza]*. Adž□pa, Cherkessk.

Johanna Mattissen. 2017. Sub-types of polysynthesis. In Michael Fortescue, Marianne Mithun, and Nicholas Evans, editors, *The Oxford Handbook of Polysynthesis*, pages 70–98. Oxford University Press.

Hyunji Hayley Park, Lane Schwartz, and Francis Tyers. 2021. Expanding Universal Dependencies for polysynthetic languages: A case of St. Lawrence Island Yupik. In *Proceedings of the First Workshop on Natural Language Processing for Indigenous Languages of the Americas*, pages 131–142, Online. Association for Computational Linguistics.

Robert Pugh, Marivel Huerta Mendez, Mitsuya Sasaki, and Francis Tyers. 2022. Universal Dependencies for western sierra Puebla Nahuatl. In *Proceedings of the Thirteenth Language Resources and Evaluation Conference*, pages 5011–5020, Marseille, France. European Language Resources Association.

Nurja T. Tabulova. 1976. *Grammatika abazinskogo yazyka. Fonetika i morfologia [A grammar of Abaza. Phonetics and morphology]*. Karachaevo-Cherkesskoe otdelenie Stavropol'skogo knizhnogo izdatel'stva, Cherkessk.

Francis Tyers and Karina Mishchenkova. 2020. Dependency annotation of noun incorporation in polysynthetic languages. In *Proceedings of the Fourth Workshop on Universal Dependencies (UDW 2020)*, pages 195–204, Barcelona, Spain (Online). Association for Computational Linguistics.

Peter Wittenburg, Hennie Brugman, Albert Russel, Alex Klassmann, and Han Sloetjes. 2006. ELAN: a professional framework for multimodality research. In *Proceedings of the Fifth International Conference on Language Resources and Evaluation (LREC'06)*, Genoa, Italy. European Language Resources Association (ELRA).

A Appendix

A.1 Data availability

The current version of the treebank is available here: `https://github.com/UniversalDependencies/UD_Abaza-ATB/tree/dev`.

A.2 List of abbreviations

1 — 1st person; 3 — 3rd person; ABS — absolutive; ADD — additive; ADV — adverbial; BEN — benefactive; CAUS — causative; CL.N — classifier of non-humans; COORD — coordination; CSL — cislocative; CVB — converb; DCL — declarative; DEF — definite; DIST — distal demonstrative; EMP — emphasis; ERG — ergative; F — feminine; H — human; HAB — habitual; IO — indirect object; IPF — imperfective; LOC — locative preverb; N — non-human; NEG — negation; NFIN — non-finite; NPST — non-past; PL — plural; PRS — present; PST — past; RE, REP — repetitive; REL — relativization; RFL — reflexive; SG — singular; TMP — temporal subordination.

Universalising Latin Universal Dependencies: a harmonisation of Latin treebanks in UD

Federica Gamba and **Daniel Zeman**
Charles University, Faculty of Mathematics and Physics,
Institute of Formal and Applied Linguistics, Prague, Czechia
gamba,zeman@ufal.mff.cuni.cz

Abstract

This paper presents the harmonisation process carried out on the five treebanks available for Latin in Universal Dependencies, with the aim of eliminating the discrepancies in their annotation styles. Indeed, this is the first issue to be addressed when parsing Latin, as significant drops in parsing accuracy on different Latin treebanks have been repeatedly observed. Latin syntactic variability surely accounts for this, but parsing results are as well affected by divergent annotation choices. By analysing where annotations differ, we propose a Python-based alignment of the five UD treebanks. Consequently, the impact of annotation choices on accuracy scores is assessed by performing parsing experiments with UDPipe and Stanza.

1 Introduction

A significant number of resources is available for Latin. With respect to syntax, notable are the five treebanks in Universal Dependencies[1] (de Marneffe et al., 2021), which represent a remarkable amount of data. Here is an overview:

- **Index Thomisticus Treebank** (ITTB) (Passarotti, 2019): encompassing texts by Thomas Aquinas (1225–1274) and other authors related to Thomas, it represents an example of philosophical Medieval Latin. It is the largest of the Latin treebanks.

- **Late Latin Charter Treebank** (LLCT) (Cecchini et al., 2020b): it consists of Early Medieval (VIII-IX century) Latin charters written in Tuscany, Italy, all representing the legal/documentary genre.

- **Perseus** (Bamman and Crane, 2011): it includes some of the most representative Classical Latin texts (e.g., by Augustus, Cicero, Vergil, Propertius, Sallust, Tacitus) of different genres. It is the smallest treebank in terms of number of tokens.

- **PROIEL** (Haug and Jøhndal, 2008): it contains most of the Vulgate New Testament translations, and selections from Caesar's *De bello Gallico*, Cicero's *Epistulae ad Atticum*, Palladius' *Opus Agriculturae* and the first book of Cicero's *De officiis* (examples of Classical Latin, yet representing different genres).

- **UDante** (Cecchini et al., 2020a): it includes literary texts (letters, treatises, poetry) by Dante Alighieri, corresponding to literary Medieval Latin (XIV century).

		train	**dev**	**test**
ITTB	sents	22,775	2,101	2,101
	words	390,785	29,888	29,842
LLCT	sents	7,289	850	884
	words	194,143	24,189	24,079
Perseus	sents	1,334	0	939
	words	18,184	0	10,954
PROIEL	sents	15,917	1,234	1,260
	words	172,133	13,939	14,091
UDante	sents	926	376	419
	words	30,441	11,611	13,451

Table 1: Size of UD Latin treebanks in v2.10.

The treebanks highly differ in terms of included texts and size (see Table 1), as well as in annotation. Indeed, despite the five treebanks all following the UD annotation guidelines, some differences in the annotation scheme persist. Specifically, the treebanks have been annotated by different teams and in different moments of the development of UD guidelines, resulting in different annotation choices. Thus, despite the remarkable effort made by the UD project, divergences can still be observed at all annotation levels, from word segmentation to

[1]See https://universaldependencies.org/.

Proceedings of the Sixth Workshop on Universal Dependencies (UDW, GURT/SyntaxFest 2023), pages 7 - 16
March 9-12, 2023 ©2023 Association for Computational Linguistics

lemmatisation, POS tags, morphology, and syntactic relations. In the present work we focus on the syntactic annotation. Our interventions mainly concern dependency relations, but comparable work will be needed also for lemmas and POS tags.

This study aims to syntactically harmonise the five Latin treebanks, as well as to assess the impact of different annotation choices on parsing accuracy. Section 2 motivates the present study. Section 3 presents an overview of the alignment process, while in Section 4 the harmonising interventions are highlighted in more detail. Section 5 reports the parsing scores on the aligned treebanks, demonstrating the impact of diverse annotations on parsing. Finally, Section 6 presents the conclusions and future research directions.

2 Related Work and Motivation

Parsing accuracy scores on Latin texts drop significantly when a model is applied to data that differ from those it was trained on. The issue is of course more general and concerns out-of-domain data, but with respect to Latin it is strongly intertwined with the issue of its syntactic variability. Indeed, spread over a span of more than two millennia and all across an area that corresponds to Europe, the Latin language has undergone a number of significant changes, which affected the syntactic layer as well. To be able to investigate genuine syntactic diversity, first we have to ask how much the observed drop in parsing performance is due to divergent annotation styles. A deeper understanding, and possibly levelling of such divergences would allow to isolate the impact of annotation choices and highlight intra-linguistic syntactic variability.

Such syntactic diversity, leading to lower parsing accuracies, has been repeatedly noted. For instance, Passarotti and Ruffolo (2010) and Ponti and Passarotti (2016) observed how performances drop when a model is employed to parse out-of-domain data, while Passarotti and Dell'Orletta (2010) dealt with the need of adapting a pre-existing parser to the specific processing of Medieval Latin. The issue of Latin variability has also been addressed in the EvaLatin campaigns (Sprugnoli et al., 2020; Sprugnoli et al., 2022), devoted to the evaluation of NLP tools for Latin.[2]

[2]So far EvaLatin has been focusing on lemmatisation, morphological analysis and POS tagging; in the future, EvaLatin campaigns will probably extend the cross-time and cross-genre sub-tasks to syntactic diversity (Sprugnoli et al., 2022).

On the other hand, the issue of inconsistent annotations is not unprecedented. Methods for inconsistency detection in treebanks have been proposed e.g. by Dickinson and Meurers (2003), Volokh and Neumann (2011), Ambati et al. (2011), de Marneffe et al. (2017), Aggarwal and Zeman (2020), and Aggarwal and Alzetta (2021).

With respect to Latin, a huge effort towards harmonisation has been made by the LiLa project[3] (Passarotti et al., 2020). Within the framework of Linguistic Linked Open Data, LiLa seeks to overcome the different lemmatisation criteria through a pivotal use of lemmas and hypolemmas in a knowledge base.

3 Alignment Process

For the alignment process we decide to model our interventions on the 2.10 version of the UDante treebank, which was released in May 2022. This choice is motivated by several factors:

- UDante is the only Latin treebank that has been annotated directly in UD, rather than being converted from another framework; conversion errors are thus ruled out.
- It is the newest Latin treebank in UD, meaning that it follows the latest version of the UD guidelines.
- It is developed by the same team as the other non-neglected[4] Latin treebanks (ITTB and LLCT); this team has also defined the UD guidelines for Latin.[5]

For all these reasons, UDante should be the Latin treebank most conforming to the current UD guidelines. Hence when aligning the annotation decisions in individual treebanks, we try to push them towards those of UDante. This should not be understood as pushing the *language* towards that of the genre, geographical location or historical period of UDante. Changes that we do are about annotation guidelines, and while some of them may address phenomena that are not present in all varieties of

[3]See `https://lila-erc.eu/`.

[4]As of the latest UD release, 2.10 (May 2022) *Neglected* is a technical label of the UD infrastructure, assigned to treebanks after three years since the oldest validation error. See the UD Validation Report at `http://quest.ms.mff.cuni.cz/udvalidator/cgi-bin/unidep/validation-report.pl`.

[5]See `https://universaldependencies.org/la/index.html#documentation`.

Latin, the guidelines would not be different for different varieties.

As mentioned in Section 2, the interventions mainly focus on dependency relations, yet not exclusively: spotted conversion and random errors are corrected, as well as some inconsistencies in terms of lemmatisation and POS tags.

As a starting point of our alignment process, we choose the treebanks' train, dev and test sets as available in their UD GitHub `dev` branch as of August 30th, 2022. The treebanks are then aligned through Python scripts, specifically designed for each treebank. To manipulate data we exploit Udapi (Popel et al., 2017), a framework providing an application programming interface for UD data. Our scripts are openly available on GitHub,[6] together with the aligned treebanks. Moreover, we are ready to contribute the harmonised treebanks to the official UD releases.

4 Treebank Investigation

An overview of the current state and our modifications of the treebanks is presented in the following subsections. Further information can be retrieved directly from the scripts available in GitHub.

4.1 Tokenisation

Although we focus on syntactic relations, some of our interventions affect other annotation levels as well. Some issues can be found already at the level of tokenisation. For instance, a form like *nobiscum* 'with us', composed of the pronoun *nobis* 'us' and the postponed, enclitic adposition *cum* 'with', is often not properly split in a multi-word token, but it is considered as a unique token. However, this entails losing the value of the preposition *cum*. Occurrences are found in ITTB, LLCT and Perseus. In ITTB and LLCT, such instances (although rare) are attached as `obl`; in Perseus, the `advmod` relation is assigned. We thus split these tokens, by assigning an `obl` relation to the pronoun, and annotating *cum* as its `case` marker.

Negative conjunctions like *neque* and *nec* 'and not' can be problematic, as happens in Perseus, where they are currently split and inverted. See e.g. *et nemo poterat in caelo* ***que ne*** *in terra* ***que ne*** *subtus terram aperire librum* ***que ne*** *respicere illum* 'And nobody in heaven, nor in earth, neither under the earth, could open the book, neither to look at it' (Bible, *Rev.* 5,3). This tokenisation does not correspond to the original text (*neque...neque...neque*), and is probably an erroneous result of the conversion from the original data.

Moreover, across the treebanks (except for LLCT and UDante) some instances are found where the abbreviation dot is not separated from the abbreviated form: e.g., *C. Rufus* in Perseus, *Kal. Ian.* in PROIEL. We thus split those occurrences into two distinct tokens.[7]

4.2 POS tags

Some interventions concerning POS tags are needed, especially as they often affect the choice of the dependency relation. A critical point in all the four treebanks (with the exception of UDante) is represented by discourse adverbs like *enim*, *igitur*, *itaque* ('indeed, therefore'), that do not constitute true adverbs but rather discourse elements reinforcing the deployment of the sentence. Often annotated as adverbs (ADV, `advmod`), they are corrected in PARTs with `discourse` deprel. The line between these two POS tags is often not clearly drawn, and the case of *o*, used to address a recipient in vocative case, proves it as well: mainly tagged as ADV in ITTB, Perseus and PROIEL, it has been reannotated as PART. No instances of *o* are found in LLCT, due to the genre of the corpus.

A general harmonisation of determiners (DET, `det`) is performed on all treebanks by defining a lexical list of determiners, modeled on those occurring in UDante. While being a shared issue, this is particularly relevant for Perseus. Indeed, the Perseus-employed tagset does not include some, quite important, tags. It is the case of AUX, DET and PART. PROPN, although officially used, is often missing. The absence of the DET tag is extremely relevant, given its widespread distribution over Latin texts. Through the lexical list, as well as through morphological accordance with parent node and after re-annotating the many determiners originally attached as `amod` or `nmod`, we assign the correct POS tag and relations.

The AUX for auxiliaries was not employed either; it is now assigned to occurrences of *sum* 'to be' with deprel `cop`, `aux` or `aux:pass`. We also retrieve proper nouns in a very trivial way, by locating capitalised nouns, since it is needed to correct

[6] `https://github.com/fjambe/Latin-variability` (commit `303acc5`).

[7] Tokenization of abbreviations is not unified UD-wide. In some languages the guideline is to keep the abbreviation with its punctuation as one token, while in others, including Latin, the punctuation should be separated.

some dependencies. Indeed, proper nouns represent a very critical point in Perseus annotation, also due to the ample variety of different combinations of nouns and proper nouns.[8] We restore correct dependencies and assign the appropriate dependency label: `flat` for a PROPN depending on a NOUN, `flat:name` to different components of a same proper noun.

In Perseus and PROIEL, we try to replace the X tag (unknown word) with the appropriate one. Some subordinating conjunctions, currently tagged as ADV, are corrected to SCONJ.

4.3 Syntax

As already mentioned, our main interventions concern dependency relations. In this regard, we replace `expl:pass` deprel—either with `obj` or `obl` according to the grammatical case of the word form—as it is not employed in UDante. Consider for instance *aliter* ***se*** *habet intellectus divinus, atque aliter intellectus noster* (lit. 'otherwise itself has intellect divine, and otherwise intellect our') 'there is a difference between the divine intellect and ours' (SCG 1, XXII, 5): `expl:pass(habet,se)` is reannotated as `obj(habet,se)`.

Compound numerals like *viginti quattuor* 'twenty-four' display various annotations in the original treebanks, representing one of the most diverging phenomena. In LLCT, the numbers are connected as `compound` with the first number as head (`compound(viginti, quattuor)`). Other treebanks use different relations: in Perseus, the numbers are connected using `nummod`, and in PROIEL, `fixed` (the first number is the head in all cases). In accordance to UD guidelines, all these dependencies are reannotated as `flat` (i.e. `flat(viginti, quattuor)`).[9]

Indirect objects (`iobj`) often occur in Perseus and PROIEL. They are replaced with `obl:arg` in the latter, and with `obl`, or `obl:arg` if in dative form, in the former. Indeed, despite the label being the same, its use in the two treebanks is not completely identical.

In ITTB some prepositions depending on the wrong head, namely on a token that precedes in the word order[10] are reassigned to their correct head, which is identified based on dependency relations and POS tags. For instance, in *Voluntas autem non* ***ex*** *necessitate fertur in ea quae sunt ad finem* (lit. 'will but not by necessity lead to those that are for a goal') 'the will is not necessarily directed to the means' (*Summa Contra Gentiles*, 1, LXXXI, 2) the parent node of both *ex* and *necessitate* was *non*. We restore the correct dependencies, resulting in `case(necessitate, ex)` and `obl(fertur, necessitate)`.

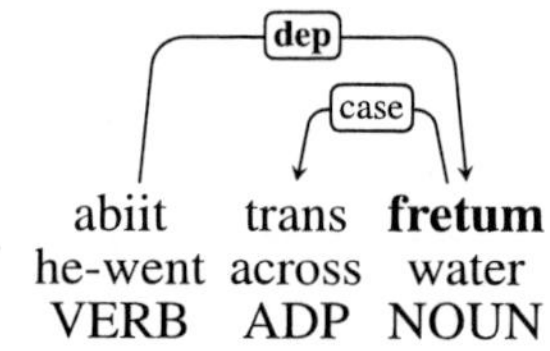

Figure 1: Example of a `dep` dependency (en. 'he departed to the other side').

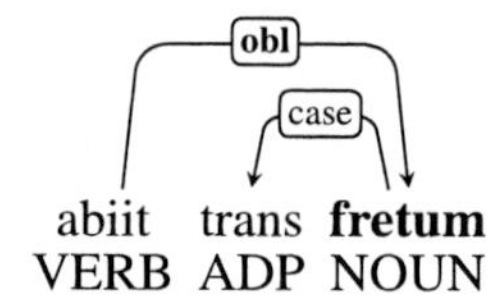

Figure 2: Result of the harmonisation process.[12]

Interestingly, PROIEL contains the `dep` relation (intended for cases where a more precise dependency type cannot be determined). Through POS tags and morphology, we replace it with a more appropriate one,[11] as illustrated in Figures 1 and 2.

Often problematic across treebanks, and in many different ways, the `advmod` deprel needs a closer inspection. In general, the dependency is improperly assigned to many non-adverbial instances. In ITTB, an interesting case is provided by biblical references, e.g. *dicitur enim hebr. 3-1* 'it is said in the letter to the Hebrews, 3-1'. The specification of the relevant Bible's book sometimes depends as `advmod` on its parent node, i.e., the predicate *dicitur* in the proposed example; we convert it into `obl`, since it is a nominal form. In Perseus, we solve the issue of non-adverbial `advmod` through different criteria: lexical ones,

[8]E.g., *Tarquinio Prisco, Q Titurium Sabinum legatum, L. Valerio Flacco et C. Pomptino praetoribus, Aemilio Papo imperatore.*

[9]Except for cases where a coordinating conjunction is present: *viginti et quattuor* is coordination, hence `conj(viginti, quattuor); cc(quattuor, et)`.

[10]Postpositions are very rare in Latin.

[11]For more detailed information, see the harmonisation script on GitHub.

[12]The most accurate dependency label would be `obl:lmod`. However, as it is difficult to assign this subtype automatically, and subtypes are ignored in current parsing scores, we just assign `obl`.

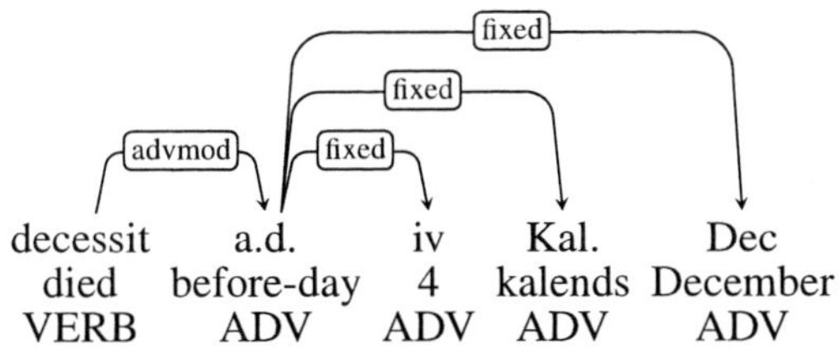

Figure 3: Annotation in UD 2.10.

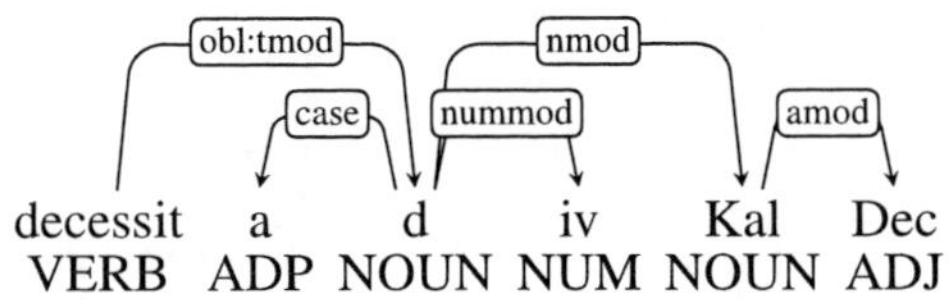

Figure 4: Result of the harmonisation process.

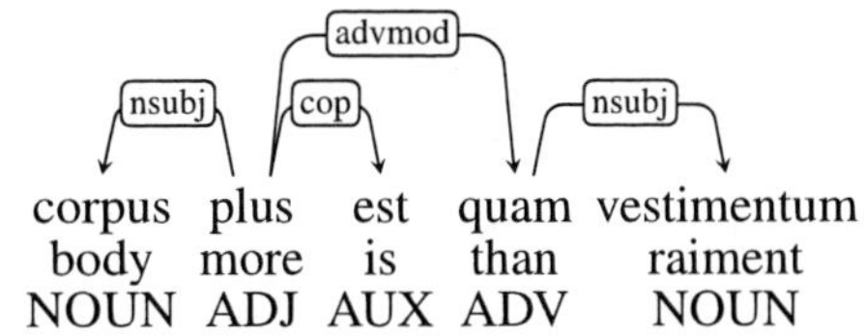

Figure 5: Annotation in UD 2.10.

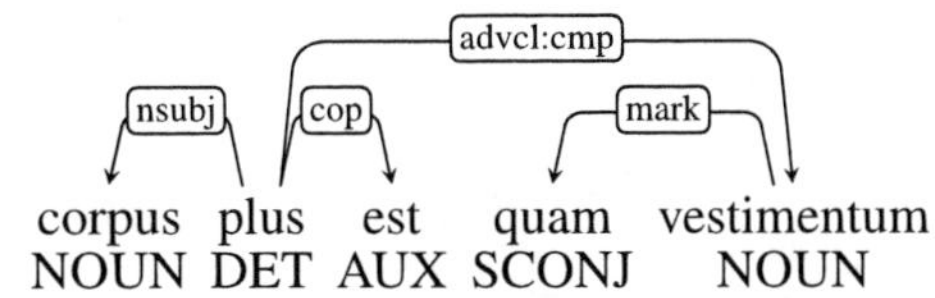

Figure 6: Result of the harmonisation process.

e.g., to all tokens with lemma *autem* 'but' deprel `cc` is assigned; morphological ones, e.g., if a substantive has `Case=Loc`, `Dat` or `Voc`, it is attached as `obl`, `obl:arg` or `vocative` respectively; and POS criteria, e.g., if a token is tagged SCONJ, it receives the `mark` relation. The same issue is found also in PROIEL. For instance, *hic a mortuis resurrexit* 'he is risen from the dead' (Jerome's Vulgate, Mark 6) is once annotated as follows: `advmod(resurrexit, mortuis)`, `case(mortuis, a)`. We thus try to restore similar occurrences of `obl`iques, and other dependencies wrongly considered adverbial.

Another example of incorrect `advmod` relations is provided by calendar expressions, often found in PROIEL data. Consider, for instance, the sentence *pater nobis decessit* ***a.d. iv Kal. Dec*** 'Our father died on November 28th' (Cicero, *Epistulae ad Atticum*, 1, 6). Before the alignment, *a.d.* (*ante diem* 'before the day') and *iv* are not properly lemmatised, as their lemmas are respectively *calendar* and *expression*, they have no morphological features, and each token of the whole phrase, including *Kal.* and *Dec*, is tagged as ADV. The relation between the date and its parent is `advmod`. The annotation is not even internally consistent: occurrences where tokens are not split, e.g. *Kal.Decembr* (lemmatised as *calendar.expression* and tagged ADV) can be found. The annotation of abbreviated dates in UD should reflect how the date would be pronounced (Zeman, 2021). However, cases like *Kal.Dec* are not straightforward, as they could be expanded in two possible ways—leading to two different analyses. The month can be either understood as an ADJ which takes a plural feminine form to agree with *kalendae/nonae/idus* (e.g., *Kalendae Decembres*), or a genitive singular (*Kalendae Decembris*). In cases where this is impossible to disambiguate, we take the first as the default reading. As far as possible, we try to align these occurrences and replace shallow labels like *calendar.expression*, as well as to assign correct dependencies (Figures 3 and 4).

In terms of coordination, the main intervention concerns reattaching conjunctions to the second conjunct instead of the first one; it is applied to Perseus and PROIEL. This is a significant change between UD v1 and v2 (Nivre et al., 2020), showing that the conversion of these treebanks to UD v2 was not perfect. Moreover, in Perseus `parataxis` is often found to be employed for coordination, and is corrected into `conj`.

A significant intervention in ITTB and LLCT applies to constructions involving the copula *sum* 'to be' and a prepositional phrase (often, but not exclusively, with locative meaning). In many such cases the copula occurs as the head, while the prepositional phrase depends on it as `obl`. Following the UD guidelines, we reverse the hierarchy by making the oblique the head and the copula its `cop` dependant. An example from ITTB: *successio autem propter motum aliquem est* (lit. 'succession however because of movement some is') 'succession results from change of some kind' (SCG 1, XCIX, 6): `obl(est, motum)` is reannotated as `cop(motum, est)`, and all the dependents of the former head (*est*), e.g. the subject *successio*, are reattached to the new one (*motum*).

Comparative clauses are often problematic across the Latin treebanks, perhaps with the exception of ITTB, where our interventions are mostly limited to subtyping the `advcl` relation to `:cmp`

	ITTB	LLCT	Perseus	PROIEL	UDante	notes
abbr	1302	-	24	107	-	split dot and abbreviated word; in PROIEL, removed dot as punctuation is missing
advcl:abs	521	2019	163	1088	-	added subtype to absolute ablatives
advcl:cmp	2582	621	59	821	-	corrected deprel for comparative clauses (often, dependencies as well)
advmod:lmod	2505	1224	56	581	27	added subtype
advmod:neg	-	624	274	2691	-	added subtype to negation
advmod:tmod	-	386	231	1099	77	added subtype
AUX	-	-	366	-	-	assigned AUX tag
aux-pass-periph	-	-	14	283	-	added subtype to periphrastic passive
dates	-	-	-	578	-	intervention on date/calendar expression; can refer to both label and dependency
dep	-	-	-	47	-	replaced `dep` with more appropriate label
DET	1206	53	2557	14225	-	assigned DET tag; most often, `det` entailed
expl:pass	335	-	-	-	-	replaced with `obj/obl`
flat-for-names	-	-	82	202	-	assigned `flat` (`flat:name` if appropriate) to PROPNs
incorrect-advmod	115	48	2086	1030	-	corrected `advmod` if assigned to non-adverbials
inversion-sum	2843	162	-	-	-	inverted head-dependent in copular constructions (both dependencies and labels)
inverted-prep	248	-	-	-	-	reattached prepositions depending on preceding node
iobj	-	-	491	5870	-	replace `iobj` with `obj/obl:arg`; `obj` used inappropriately (in Perseus) included
j-i	-	-	345	-	-	substituted *j* with *i* to normalise lemmas
mwt	44	28	20	60	-	split a token into multi-word token
nec	-	-	55	-	-	corrected *c ne* →*ne c*
nsubj:pass	2	-	428	338	27	added subtype to subjects of passive verbs
num	60	61	29	40	-	corrected numerals; mostly label, sometimes also dependency
parataxis-to-conj	-	-	159	-	-	`parataxis` used for coordination is replaced with `conj`
PART	7198	203	179	2254	10	assigned PART tag instead of incorrect ones (mostly ADV); negation counted separately

Table 2: Count of harmonising interventions.

for standards of comparison, as in ***ut*** *supra* ***ostensum*** *est* 'as we have proved above'. In Perseus and PROIEL, and less in LLCT, various incorrect annotation patterns can be spotted. An example from PROIEL is provided in Figures 5 and 6. In PROIEL, relative clauses present some issues as well. See for instance *ea quae sunt his similia* 'those things that are similar to these' (Cicero, *De officis*, 1, 17): *similia* should depend on *ea* as `acl:relcl`, whereas it occurs as `appos`.

An unusual annotation pattern, observed in PROIEL with respect to adverbial clauses, is exemplified by the sentence hereafter: ***postea quam*** *agros et cultum et copias Gallorum homines feri ac barbari* ***adamassent*** *traductos plures* 'after that these wild and savage men had become enamored of the lands and the refinement and the abundance of the Gauls, more were brought over' (Caesar, *De bello Gallico*, 1.31). The parent node of *adamassent*, predicate of the adverbial clause, should be the `root` *traductos*, and its deprel `advcl`, while the subordinating conjunction *quam* 'that' should be its child node with `mark` dependency relation. However, in the original annotation we observe `fixed(quam, adamassent)` and `advcl(traductos, quam)`.

In some cases, dependency relations are lacking subtypes. Although the current parsing evaluation does not take them into account (see Section 5), we still believe that it is useful to unify them, also in view of more detailed work in the future. Therefore, for adverbs we identify a list[13] of locative and temporal adverbs, and mark them with the `lmod` and `tmod` subtypes. This applies to all the five treebanks, UDante included. Indeed, in UDante locative and temporal adverbs (`advmod`) are already marked; yet, since in some cases the subtypes are missing, we assign them using the lexical list. Similarly, in the other four treebanks relative clauses and absolute ablatives respectively receive the sub-

[13]The list is not intended to be exhaustive in the present stage of the research.

types `relcl` and `abs`, if missing. In Perseus and PROIEL, the same applies to negations, which are assigned the `advmod:neg` dependency relation.

4.4 Summary

The investigation reveals recurring issues which are spread across all treebanks (Table 2), although differing in various ways. The most widespread issues are the `tmod` and `lmod` relation subtypes, as well as comparative clauses.

However, more interventions are needed in Perseus and PROIEL than in the other three treebanks. Indeed, the degree of accordance with the UD guidelines is definitely lower in the Perseus treebank—perhaps unsurprisingly, as it has not been updated since its initial conversion to UD v2 in 2017. PROIEL's condition resembles that of Perseus, including the status of *neglected* in the latest release (May 2022).

Only minor modifications are needed in UDante, which comes as no surprise, as this treebank was selected as the reference point for the whole harmonisation process. Overall, the main divergence between UDante and the other treebanks lies in relation subtypes. Indeed, UDante employs a range of subtypes that is not shared by the other treebanks, and that would be problematic if the parsing evaluation process included subtypes;[14] since it is currently not the case (Section 5), we choose not to focus on this specific issue.

5 Impact on Parsing

Afterwards, we try to assess the impact that a harmonised annotation of the five treebanks has on parsing accuracy. In order to achieve this, with both UDPipe and Stanza we retrain a model for every aligned treebank. We then test the obtained models on each of the treebanks; Tables 4 and 6 summarise the scores, in terms of Labeled Attachment Score (LAS) and Unlabeled Attachment Score (UAS) (Buchholz and Marsi, 2006), obtained with models trained with UDPipe and Stanza respectively. To measure accuracy, we employ the Python evaluation script[15] designed for the CoNLL 2018 Shared Task on Multilingual Parsing from Raw Text to Universal Dependencies (Zeman et al., 2018). As mentioned earlier, the script takes into account only main dependency types, without considering subtypes. This reflects our current needs; nevertheless, the present treebank alignment is only the first stage of a larger harmonisation effort, and additional evaluation criteria (including relation subtypes) can be introduced in the future.

To demonstrate the effect of harmonisation, we also present LAS and UAS scores of models trained on pre-harmonisation data (Tables 3 and 5), again with UDPipe and Stanza. Such models are trained and tested on `master` data of Universal Dependencies 2.10, officially released in May 2022.

Both series of models, pre- and post-alignment, are trained with the same settings. With respect to UDPipe, version 1.2 is used; we employ pretrained fastText embeddings[16] (Grave et al., 2018) and optimised training hyperparameters as described for reproducible training by Straka and Straková (2019), within the publication of UD 2.5 models for UDPipe. Since optimised hyperparameters are available only for ITTB, Perseus and PROIEL, for LLCT and UDante we experiment with different options and select the best ones.[17] As for pre-alignment models for Stanza, we employ the ITTB, Perseus and PROIEL models made available[18] by the Stanza team and pretrained on UD 2.8, since those treebanks did not change afterwards, as reported in their change log. We train pre-alignment models for LLCT and UDante, as well as all post-alignment ones, with default parameters and fastText embeddings.

Some conclusions can be drawn from the comparison of the tables. With UDPipe, the interventions prove effective in most cases, as models trained on harmonised treebanks reach higher scores than the pre-alignment ones. This holds true especially with respect to results on Perseus and PROIEL; indeed, each of the post-alignment models gains higher scores on these two treebanks. The improvement is substantial (up to +9% with more than one model), and confirms once more the absolute relevance of a truly universal annotation style. Higher impact on Perseus and PROIEL is expected, given their previous condition (Section 4).

Analogously, the models trained on harmonised

[14] It would also be problematic if a parser were trained jointly on concatenated Latin treebanks.

[15] Available at `https://github.com/UniversalDependencies/tools/blob/master/eval.py`.

[16] Available at `https://fasttext.cc/docs/en/crawl-vectors.html`.

[17] LLCT: learning_rate=0.02, transition_system=swap, transition_oracle=static_lazy, structured_interval=8.

UDante: learning_rate=0.01, transition_system=projective, transition_oracle=dynamic, structured_interval=8.

[18] At `https://stanfordnlp.github.io/stanza/available_models.html`.

	ittb.udp		llct.udp		perseus.udp		proiel.udp		udante.udp	
	LAS	UAS	LAS	UAS	LAS	UAS	LAS	UAS	LAS	UAS
ITTB	**84.51%**	**86.23%**	44.25%	52.16%	29.54%	40.56%	30.54%	45.43%	59.93%	65.77%
LLCT	44.22%	50.16%	**93.02%**	**93.85%**	28.92%	37.44%	40.37%	52.10%	45.57%	53.42%
Perseus	33.28%	44.21%	39.85%	48.71%	**61.80%**	**67.18%**	38.93%	55.16%	35.64%	45.79%
PROIEL	39.10%	50.86%	43.16%	53.08%	41.52%	52.36%	**73.51%**	**77.45%**	39.43%	48.62%
UDante	50.78%	58.51%	36.95%	45.78%	22.44%	32.41%	26.72%	40.41%	**50.81%**	**57.32%**

Table 3: UDPipe scores before treebank alignment. Columns correspond to trained models, rows to test data.

	ittb.udp		llct.udp		perseus.udp		proiel.udp		udante.udp	
	LAS	UAS	LAS	UAS	LAS	UAS	LAS	UAS	LAS	UAS
ITTB	**83.83%**	**85.51%**	43.80%	51.45%	43.17%	53.12%	40.46%	51.33%	61.68%	67.39%
LLCT	43.12%	48.55%	**93.11%**	**93.88%**	47.31%	54.13%	46.69%	55.23%	41.56%	49.05%
Perseus	42.73%	53.54%	48.69%	55.24%	**63.80%**	**68.38%**	49.98%	59.25%	43.59%	54.23%
PROIEL	46.77%	55.39%	50.37%	57.48%	53.11%	59.88%	**75.78%**	**78.87%**	46.13%	55.15%
UDante	53.06%	59.95%	38.51%	46.69%	35.59%	45.64%	30.72%	44.11%	**54.50%**	**61.02%**

Table 4: UDPipe scores after treebank alignment. Columns correspond to trained models, rows to test data.

Perseus and PROIEL achieve better scores on every of the five treebanks. Peaks are represented by LLCT parsed with a Perseus model (around +17% both in LAS and UAS). As for PROIEL, the increases are slightly lower, yet still substantial. Consider, for instance, the performance of a PROIEL post-alignment model on Perseus test data: an improvement of +11 percentage points is assessed with respect to LAS.

The model trained on aligned UDante proves to gain higher scores on almost every treebank,[19] with more substantial increases on Perseus and PROIEL. This is mostly due to the alignment interventions on the other treebanks than on UDante itself, as the harmonisation process was minimal on UDante data. The increase observed when a UDante model is employed to parse UDante test data could be probably caused by divergences between release 2.10 of UDante, which the model in Table 3 was trained on, and UDante `dev` data, used as the basis for the alignment.

ITTB and LLCT models show a less consistent behaviour, performing sometimes better (i.e. on Perseus and PROIEL), sometimes marginally worse (e.g. ITTB model on ITTB and LLCT test data). A closer analysis of the parser outputs, despite not providing a precise explanation for the parser behaviour, reveals that the harmonisation can be further enhanced. For instance, it emerges that the harmonisation of copular constructions, as discussed in Subsection 4.3,[20] did not catch all occurrences and the wrong original annotation survives in some sentences. Such coexistence of pre- and post-harmonisation annotations, and thus a lower degree of consistency, may partially explain the observed decrease in parsing accuracy.

The general trend of improved scores can be observed also when models are trained with Stanza. Yet, the increase is not as considerable as when UDPipe is employed.

However, Tables 3, 5, 4 and 6 also highlight how the treebank annotation alignment does not solve the issue discussed in Section 2: the drop is still significant when data are parsed with models trained on a different treebank. Moreover, the absolute scores presented depend also on the size of training data, which varies substantially across the treebanks (see Table 1), Perseus being particularly small.

6 Conclusion and Future Work

The annotation alignment proposed in the present paper confirms the relevance of a shared and universal annotation scheme. Thus, although the Universal Dependencies project already represents an outstanding milestone, the effort needed in this direction is still remarkable, and two-fold: on the one hand, treebanks should be constantly updated to the latest UD guidelines, as they keep developing towards a more consistent annotation formalism. On the other hand, different research teams working on the same language should collaboratively define shared guidelines and adopt the same approach in annotation, so that Universal Dependencies can grow more and more *universal*.

Many future directions can be envisaged for this study. The alignment needs to be further inves-

[19] LLCT represents an exception.

[20] See the example from ITTB: *Successio autem propter motum aliquem est.*

	`ittb.mdl`		`llct.mdl`		`perseus.mdl`		`proiel.mdl`		`udante.mdl`	
	LAS	UAS	LAS	UAS	LAS	UAS	LAS	UAS	LAS	UAS
ITTB	**89.16%**	**91.26%**	47.27%	60.00%	45.99%	59.32%	44.49%	60.37%	60.80%	70.37%
LLCT	47.57%	58.79%	**94.56%**	**95.78%**	29.38%	46.17%	38.34%	51.77%	41.96%	53.54%
Perseus	51.31%	65.56%	34.33%	49.73%	**61.65%**	**71.35%**	45.19%	61.89%	44.26%	59.71%
PROIEL	54.53%	68.10%	40.70%	56.06%	48.25%	65.42%	**79.80%**	**84.17%**	44.83%	57.75%
UDante	57.07%	68.44%	39.16%	52.88%	32.09%	48.42%	37.21%	50.32%	**56.84%**	**66.12%**

Table 5: Stanza scores before treebank alignment. Columns correspond to trained models, rows to test data.

	`ittb.mdl`		`llct.mdl`		`perseus.mdl`		`proiel.mdl`		`udante.mdl`	
	LAS	UAS	LAS	UAS	LAS	UAS	LAS	UAS	LAS	UAS
ITTB	**88.60%**	**90.55%**	45.63%	58.74%	50.55%	61.47%	51.16%	60.72%	63.78%	72.96%
LLCT	40.84%	52.66%	**94.61%**	**95.81%**	37.82%	47.50%	40.97%	53.24%	43.64%	56.09%
Perseus	57.68%	67.85%	40.80%	53.88%	**58.41%**	**68.22%**	47.30%	58.68%	52.98%	64.06%
PROIEL	62.34%	71.27%	46.76%	59.92%	55.03%	65.25%	**80.57%**	**84.36%**	52.61%	63.91%
UDante	56.62%	67.27%	39.67%	52.97%	39.53%	52.98%	41.27%	52.41%	**57.92%**	**67.60%**

Table 6: Stanza scores after treebank alignment. Columns correspond to trained models, rows to test data.

tigated, not only at the level of tokenisation and dependency relations, but also with respect to lemmatisation, POS tagging and morphological features. In the near future, we plan to test some error detection methods in order to locate annotation inconsistencies within and among the five treebanks and intervene on them. See Section 2 for some preliminary references.

Moreover, we intend to carry out an error analysis of automatically parsed treebanks, so as to identify some error trends, and possibly compare parsing errors before and after treebank alignment.

Once the treebanks follow a more uniform annotation style, it will be possible and appropriate to investigate the actual linguistic differences causing performance drops when models trained on one treebank are applied to another. Possible directions for this future work include an analysis of genre diversity, a closer examination of different types of employed embeddings, and exploitation of Latin BERT (Bamman and Burns, 2020). The results could lead to the definition of strategies to overcome the issue of Latin syntactic variability.

Acknowledgements

This work was supported by the Grant No. 20-16819X (LUSyD) of the Czech Science Foundation (GAČR) and by the GAUK project "Syntactic parsing of Latin texts – dealing with linguistic diversity".

References

Akshay Aggarwal and Chiara Alzetta. 2021. Atypical or underrepresented? A pilot study on small treebanks. In *Proceedings of the Eighth Italian Conference on Computational Linguistics, CLiC-it 2021, Milan, Italy, January 26-28, 2022*, volume 3033 of *CEUR Workshop Proceedings*. CEUR-WS.org.

Akshay Aggarwal and Daniel Zeman. 2020. Estimating POS annotation consistency of different treebanks in a language. In *Proceedings of the 19th International Workshop on Treebanks and Linguistic Theories*, pages 93–110, Düsseldorf, Germany. Association for Computational Linguistics.

Bharat Ram Ambati, Rahul Agarwal, Mridul Gupta, Samar Husain, and Dipti Misra Sharma. 2011. Error detection for treebank validation. In *Proceedings of the 9th Workshop on Asian Language Resources*, pages 23–30, Chiang Mai, Thailand. Asian Federation of Natural Language Processing.

David Bamman and Patrick J. Burns. 2020. Latin BERT: A contextual language model for classical philology. *CoRR*, abs/2009.10053.

David Bamman and Gregory Crane. 2011. The Ancient Greek and Latin Dependency Treebanks. In *Language technology for cultural heritage*, pages 79–98. Springer.

Sabine Buchholz and Erwin Marsi. 2006. CoNLL-X shared task on multilingual dependency parsing. In *Proceedings of the Tenth Conference on Computational Natural Language Learning (CoNLL-X)*, pages 149–164, New York City. Association for Computational Linguistics.

Flavio M Cecchini, Rachele Sprugnoli, Giovanni Moretti, and Marco Passarotti. 2020a. UDante: First Steps Towards the Universal Dependencies Treebank of Dante's Latin Works. In *Seventh Italian Conference on Computational Linguistics*, pages 1–7. CEUR Workshop Proceedings.

Flavio Massimiliano Cecchini, Timo Korkiakangas, and Marco Passarotti. 2020b. A New Latin Treebank for Universal Dependencies: Charters between Ancient Latin and Romance Languages. In *Proceedings of the 12th Language Resources and Evaluation*

Conference, Marseille, France. European Language Resources Association.

Marie-Catherine de Marneffe, Matias Grioni, Jenna Kanerva, and Filip Ginter. 2017. Assessing the annotation consistency of the Universal Dependencies corpora. In *Proceedings of the Fourth International Conference on Dependency Linguistics (Depling 2017)*, pages 108–115, Pisa,Italy. Linköping University Electronic Press.

Marie-Catherine de Marneffe, Christopher Manning, Joakim Nivre, and Daniel Zeman. 2021. Universal Dependencies. *Computational Linguistics*, 47(2):255–308.

Markus Dickinson and W Detmar Meurers. 2003. Detecting inconsistencies in treebanks. In *Proceedings of TLT*, volume 3, pages 45–56.

Edouard Grave, Piotr Bojanowski, Prakhar Gupta, Armand Joulin, and Tomas Mikolov. 2018. Learning word vectors for 157 languages. In *Proceedings of the Eleventh International Conference on Language Resources and Evaluation (LREC 2018)*, Miyazaki, Japan. European Language Resources Association (ELRA).

Dag TT Haug and Marius Jøhndal. 2008. Creating a Parallel Treebank of the Old Indo-European Bible Translations. In *Proceedings of the Second Workshop on Language Technology for Cultural Heritage Data (LaTeCH 2008)*, pages 27–34.

Joakim Nivre, Marie-Catherine de Marneffe, Filip Ginter, Jan Hajič, Christopher D. Manning, Sampo Pyysalo, Sebastian Schuster, Francis Tyers, and Daniel Zeman. 2020. Universal Dependencies v2: An evergrowing multilingual treebank collection. In *Proceedings of the Twelfth Language Resources and Evaluation Conference*, pages 4034–4043, Marseille, France. European Language Resources Association.

Marco Passarotti. 2019. The Project of the Index Thomisticus Treebank. *Digital Classical Philology*, 10:299–320.

Marco Passarotti and Felice Dell'Orletta. 2010. Improvements in parsing the index Thomisticus treebank. revision, combination and a feature model for medieval Latin. In *Proceedings of the Seventh International Conference on Language Resources and Evaluation (LREC'10)*, Valletta, Malta. European Language Resources Association (ELRA).

Marco Passarotti, Francesco Mambrini, Greta Franzini, Flavio Massimiliano Cecchini, Eleonora Litta, Giovanni Moretti, Paolo Ruffolo, and Rachele Sprugnoli. 2020. Interlinking through lemmas. The lexical collection of the LiLa knowledge base of linguistic resources for Latin. *Linguistic Studies and Essays*, 58(1):177–212.

Marco Passarotti and Paolo Ruffolo. 2010. Parsing the Index Thomisticus Treebank. Some Preliminary Results. In *15th International Colloquium on Latin Linguistics*, pages 714—725. Innsbrucker Beiträge zur Sprachwissenschaft.

Edoardo Maria Ponti and Marco Passarotti. 2016. Differentia compositionem facit. a slower-paced and reliable parser for Latin. In *Proceedings of the Tenth International Conference on Language Resources and Evaluation (LREC'16)*, pages 683–688, Portorož, Slovenia. European Language Resources Association (ELRA).

Martin Popel, Zdeněk Žabokrtský, and Martin Vojtek. 2017. Udapi: Universal API for Universal Dependencies. In *Proceedings of the NoDaLiDa 2017 Workshop on Universal Dependencies (UDW 2017)*, pages 96–101, Gothenburg, Sweden. Association for Computational Linguistics.

Rachele Sprugnoli, Marco Passarotti, Flavio Massimiliano Cecchini, Margherita Fantoli, and Giovanni Moretti. 2022. Overview of the EvaLatin 2022 evaluation campaign. In *Proceedings of the Second Workshop on Language Technologies for Historical and Ancient Languages*, pages 183–188, Marseille, France. European Language Resources Association.

Rachele Sprugnoli, Marco Passarotti, Flavio Massimiliano Cecchini, and Matteo Pellegrini. 2020. Overview of the EvaLatin 2020 evaluation campaign. In *Proceedings of LT4HALA 2020 - 1st Workshop on Language Technologies for Historical and Ancient Languages*, pages 105–110, Marseille, France. European Language Resources Association (ELRA).

Milan Straka and Jana Straková. 2019. Universal dependencies 2.5 models for UDPipe (2019-12-06). LINDAT/CLARIAH-CZ digital library at the Institute of Formal and Applied Linguistics (ÚFAL), Faculty of Mathematics and Physics, Charles University.

Alexander Volokh and Günter Neumann. 2011. Automatic detection and correction of errors in dependency treebanks. In *Proceedings of the 49th Annual Meeting of the Association for Computational Linguistics: Human Language Technologies*, pages 346–350, Portland, Oregon, USA. Association for Computational Linguistics.

Daniel Zeman. 2021. Date and time in Universal Dependencies. In *Proceedings of the Fifth Workshop on Universal Dependencies (UDW, SyntaxFest 2021)*, pages 173–193, Sofia, Bulgaria. Association for Computational Linguistics.

Daniel Zeman, Jan Hajič, Martin Popel, Martin Potthast, Milan Straka, Filip Ginter, Joakim Nivre, and Slav Petrov. 2018. CoNLL 2018 shared task: Multilingual parsing from raw text to Universal Dependencies. In *Proceedings of the CoNLL 2018 Shared Task: Multilingual Parsing from Raw Text to Universal Dependencies*, pages 1–21, Brussels, Belgium. Association for Computational Linguistics.

Sinhala Dependency Treebank (STB)

Chamila Liyanage[*], **Kengatharaiyer Sarveswaran**[+], **Thilini Nadungodage**[*] and **Randil Pushpananda**[*]

[*]University of Colombo School of Computing, Sri Lanka
[*]{cml,hnd,rpn}@ucsc.cmb.ac.lk
[+]Department of Computer Science, University of Jaffna, Sri Lanka
[+]sarves@univ.jfn.ac.lk

Abstract

This paper reports the development of the first dependency treebank for the Sinhala language (STB). Sinhala, which is morphologically rich, is a low-resource language with few linguistic and computational resources available publicly. This treebank consists of 100 sentences taken from a large contemporary written text corpus. These sentences were annotated manually according to the Universal Dependencies framework. In this paper, apart from elaborating on the approach that has been followed to create the treebank, we have also discussed some interesting syntactic constructions found in the corpus and how we have handled them using the current Universal Dependencies specification.

1 Introduction

Integrating linguistic information, specifically syntactic information, into language processing tools and applications improves accuracy. This has been proven for applications such as machine translators (Habash, 2007; Li et al., 2017) and natural language understanding (McCord et al., 2012; Ohta et al., 2006). It is also shown that explicitly integrating syntactic and semantic information for training pre-trained models such as Bidirectional Encoder Representations from Transformer (BERT) improves the model's performance (Zhou et al., 2020), even though some of the linguistic information will automatically be learned during the model training. This constitutes evidence that data annotated with syntactic information are essential for the development of NLP applications. In addition, linguists also use linguistically annotated data and computational tools to do linguistic analysis. Therefore, they also require linguistic resources.

Like other Indic languages (Bhattacharyya et al., 2019), Sinhala is also a low-resource language with a few publicly available resources. de Silva (2019) has surveyed available tools and resources in the Sinhala language and reported that no parsers or syntactically annotated treebanks are available for Sinhala. However, some Parts of Speech (POS) and Name Entity Recognition (NER) data are available. In addition, other resources like parallel corpora (Guzmán et al., 2019; Fernando et al., 2022) are also available.

This paper reports the development of the first-ever treebank with syntactic annotations for the Sinhala language. These annotations are added according to the Universal Dependencies framework.

2 The Sinhala Language

The Sinhala language is an Indo-Aryan language spoken by about 20 million people worldwide. It is one of the two official languages in Sri Lanka, spoken by 75% of its population. Tamil, Sanskrit and Pali have influenced the Sinhala language. Although Tamil is from a different language family called Dravidian, Sinhala has been in contact with it for a long time. The Portuguese, the Dutch, and the English colonized and stayed in Sri Lanka for centuries. Therefore, the influence of the languages spoken by them can be seen in Sinhala; several daily words have been borrowed from Portuguese and Dutch. Further, Sinhala has linguistic similarities with languages like Hindi, Bengali, Panjabi, and Marathi *etc.* spoken in India and Divehi, which is primarily spoken in the Maldives.

Sinhala is a diglossic language which appears in two distinct varieties: Spoken Sinhala and Written Sinhala, also known as Colloquial Sinhala and Literary Sinhala, respectively. Significant differences in these two styles are marked in all levels of the language, including lexical and syntactic levels (Gair, 1968). Sinhala is a relatively free word order language, though its unmarked word order is SOV. Different word orders are also possible with discourse–pragmatic effects (Liyanage et al., 2012). As with most Indo-Aryan languages,

Proceedings of the Sixth Workshop on Universal Dependencies (UDW, GURT/SyntaxFest 2023), pages 17 - 26
March 9-12, 2023 ©2023 Association for Computational Linguistics

Sinhala is also an agglutinative language in which a single nominal element can be inflected for several forms to indicate the grammatical features of the case, number, gender, definiteness and animacy, and a verbal element can be conjugated for that of tense, number, gender, person, and volition (Karunatillake, 2009).

Although no work is reportedly done on developing a treebank for Sinhala, Liyanage and Wijeratne (2017) have discussed a dependency-based annotation schema for the Sinhala language, which has not proceeded to develop a treebank. Further, Prasanna (2021) has also analyzed the dependency relations of the Sinhala language from a theoretical perspective.

3 Treebank Development

In this section, we have outlined the steps we followed to create the Sinhala treebank.

3.1 Our approach

In accordance with the Universal Dependencies (UD), the treebank annotation includes lemma, POS, morphological features, and dependency relations. The sentence annotation is performed manually, with the authors serving as the primary annotators. The process of creating the annotated treebank involved the following steps.

1. Data for the annotation was selected from a Sinhala text corpus.
2. Selected data were preprocessed and tokenized.
3. An annotation guideline was developed by considering the peculiarities of Sinhala.
4. POS, Morphology, and Dependency annotations were done manually.
5. Identified issues in the annotation were reanalyzed and fixed.
6. A conversion tool specifically developed for this work was used to provide Latin transliteration for all sentences.

When designing the annotation guideline, we referred to the dependency-based annotation schema developed for the Sinhala language (Liyanage and Wijeratne, 2017) and Indian languages (Begum et al., 2008). Further, we referred to a couple of treebanks, including Hindi Treebank (HDTB) (Tandon et al., 2016), Modern Written Tamil Treebank (MWTT) (Krishnamurthy and Sarveswaran, 2021), and Marathi Treebank (UFAL) (Ravishankar, 2017).

3.2 Data Selection

The sentences for the development of the treebank were selected from the 10 million words contemporary text corpus of UCSC. This corpus contains literary or written Sinhala texts, including novels and short stories by renowned Sinhala writers. Further, it includes Sinhala translations, critiques, and texts from mainstream Sinhala newspapers such as Silumina, Dinamina, Lankadeepa, and Lakbima. Therefore, this corpus can be considered a collection of contemporary written Sinhala and thus selected as the primary source to extract and select a set of sentences.

In the sentence selection process, the first step was to categorize all the sentences in the corpus based on the number of words in each sentence. Concise entries of one to five-word entries in the corpus are mostly the newspaper headings and topics of the writings, which cannot be considered complete sentences. Further, based on a corpus study on the UCSC's 10M word corpus, Prasanna (2021) reports that the average sentence length of Sinhala sentences is 8 to 10 words, and thus in this work, we only considered the sentences with 6 to 10 words. As a first step, we selected 500 such sentences, then eliminated colloquial and erroneous sentences to filter 100 sentences to be annotated with the UD annotations.

3.3 Word Segmentation and Lemmatization

Word segmentation is a challenge in the Sinhala writing system. This has been discussed among Sinhala linguists for decades and reported in several reforms from 1959 to 2015. The issue is still not fully resolved, and writers use varying styles in their writing. For instance, according to the word segmentation reform by the Educational Publications Department of Sri Lanka (EPD, 2014), the particle ය (ya) occurs in the finite verbs should be written without any spaces. Contrarily, it should be written separately as per the reform by the National Institute of Education (NIE, 2015). Thus, the lexical entry ගියේය *giyēya* is correct in accordance with the reform by EPD (2014); in contrast, it is incorrect, and ගියේ ය *giyē ya*, the form segmented is correct according to the reform by NIE (2015). However, in accordance with the statistics of the UCSC's 10 million words Sinhala text corpus, ගියේය *giyēya* shows 2,341 occurrences, whereas ගියේ ය *giyē ya* occurs for 2,666 times. Therefore, both lexical entries should be preserved and represented. Further, data for annotation were extracted from a text corpus, and it is worth keeping the original text as it occurs in the corpus. Accordingly, we did not follow any reforms and kept the sentences without tokenization.

Lemmatization in Sinhala is also challenging as the language is rich in morphology. When morpho-phonemic changes happen in words, it is tough to identify the lemma of a particular word. For instance, the Sinhala verb root කර *kara* 'do' becomes කරයි *karaji* do.non-past.3sg and කරති *karati* do.non-past.3pl, where markers suffixed to the lemma. However, when the verb becomes past the respective forms, become කළේය *kaḷēya* and කළෝය *kaḷōya* where the verb root has become කළ *kaḷa*. Therefore, the regular suffix stripping will not always work for Sinhala like in other morphologically rich Indic languages.

3.4 Sinhala Script and Transliteration

Sinhala script is an abugida or alphasyllabary script in which consonant-vowel sequences are written as single units, and the script is written from left to right. The script consists of 20 vowels and 40 consonants. Although the old Sinhala writing system uses some complex character combinations, in this research, we use only the character combinations used in the contemporary Sinhala writing system. Further, in the annotation, we followed the ISO 15919 standard to do the transliteration of text. In order to do this, we created a script[1].

3.5 Part-of-Speech Tagging

Although there are 17 tags in the Universal Parts-of-Speech (POS) tagset, we have used 13 POS tags in this treebank. There were no occurrences of INTJ (interjection), SCONJ (subordinating conjunction), SYM (symbol), and X (other) found in our data. The distribution of the POS tags in the treebank is given in Table 1.

[1]The tool is available at the `https://subasa.lk/` website and can be accessed through the following URL - `https://subasa.lk/services/si_en_transliteration/Real_Time_Transliteration.html`

POS Label	Count	%
ADJ	50	5.7
ADP	24	2.7
ADV	36	4.1
AUX	47	5.3
CCONJ	6	0.7
DET	23	2.6
NOUN	308	35.0
NUM	4	0.5
PART	93	10.6
PRON	44	5.0
PROPN	38	4.3
PUNCT	100	11.4
VERB	107	12.2

Table 1: Distribution of POS tags in the treebank.

3.6 Morphological Features

As a morphologically rich agglutinative language, significant linguistic information are stacked in the morphology of a word in Sinhala. We have done this annotation manually in the treebank. Morphological verb features include mood, tense, aspect, voice, evident, polarity, person, and verb form. We include the morphological features of gender, number, case, definiteness, and degree for nouns. Although animacy is not a common grammatical feature in Sinhala, it can change the morphological suffix used to mark the definiteness. Therefore, we have incorporated animacy as a feature for nouns.

For adjectives, we use degree, verbForm and tense as features. Since Sinhala is a head-final language, no relative clauses occur in the language. Instead, participial forms occur in clausal modifiers, and the head of such constructions, which we treat as adjectives, were adopted features of verbform and tense. Further, the features of number, case, gender, and person were adopted for `PronType`.

The current version of the treebank consists of 54 unique morphological feature pairs, and the feature-value pairs that have more than 50 occurrences are tabulated in Table 2.

3.7 Syntactic Annotation

Syntactic annotations also were done manually based on the annotation guideline and the previous work. However, we faced some challenges when identifying dependency relations, which are elaborated on in the following sections. As shown in

Feature	Value	Count	%
Number	Sing	229	12.4
Gender	Neut	210	11.4
Case	Nom	175	9.5
Definite	Def	140	7.6
Case	Acc	99	5.4
AdpType	Post	94	5.1
VerbForm	Fin	68	3.7
Number	Plur	65	3.5
Mood	Ind	62	3.4
VerbForm	Part	55	3.0
Gender	Masc	54	2.9
Definite	Ind	51	2.8

Table 2: List of top morphological feature-value pairs that have more than 50 occurrences in the treebank.

Table 3, the treebank consists of 24 syntactic relations out of 37 relations that are documented in the Universal Dependencies specification. Apart from these 24 primary relations, ten sub-relations have also been identified in the data. It is interesting to note that there are more nominal subjects than the given sentences. Also, a significant number of *compound:lvc* relations are also found in the treebank. This may be due to the fact that a significant number of verbs are formed from nouns by adding a verbaliser. However, this requires more linguistic analysis. Further, there are also a significant number of *nmod* found as Sinhala. Annotation of extended dependency features will be done in the future.

3.8 Head Initial vs Head Final

Sinhala is considered a head-final language, which means that the head of a phrase or sentence appears last. However, in flat multi-word expressions, the semantic head appears first in Sinhala, whereas it comes last in English. For example, in the Sinhala phrase සුමිත් මහතා *sumit mahatā*, සුමිත් *sumit* is the semantic head and appears first, while මහතා *mahatā* appears last. In contrast, in the English equivalent "Mr. Sumith" the semantic head "Sumith" appears last, while the honorific noun "Mr." appears first. In the context of this work, the head-final approach is used for some constructions, while the head-first approach is applied specifically to flat names and complex predicates.

DEPREL Label	Count	%
nsubj	109	12.4
punct	100	11.4
root	100	11.4
dep	69	7.8
case	53	6.0
nmod	53	6.0
advmod	43	4.9
obj	42	4.8
aux	38	4.3
amod	36	4.1
compound	29	3.3
det	24	2.7
obl	24	2.7
flat	19	2.2
csubj	17	1.9
acl	16	1.8
cc	6	0.7
conj	3	0.3
cop	2	0.2
mark	2	0.2
xcomp	2	0.2
advcl	1	0.1
ccomp	1	0.1
nummod	1	0.1
compound:lvc	39	4.4
compound:svc	14	1.6
nmod:poss	11	1.3
obl:lmod	10	1.1
obl:tmod	9	1.0
compound:prt	3	0.3
advmod:emph	1	0.1
aux:pass	1	0.1
det:poss	1	0.1
nmod:tmod	1	0.1

Table 3: Distribution of dependency relations in the treebank.

Occurrence type	LVC	SVC	Com
CP Finite verbs	28	09	02
CP Gerunds	09	00	00
CP Participles	06	00	00
CP With No WS	08	02	00

Table 4: CP occurrences in the treebank.

Sentence type	Count
S with non-complex predicates	26
S with complex predicates	41
S with non-verbal predicates	33

Table 5: Types of predication in the treebank

4 Discussions

This section outlines some of the interesting syntactic constructions found in the treebank. Some of these may not be common in other languages.

4.1 Predicates in Sinhala

Many of the sentences in this treebank are with a verbal predicate. As mentioned in the distribution of sentences in Table 5, 67 sentences are with verbal predicates. However, only 26 of these are with simple verbs, whereas the rest of the 41 sentences consist of complex predicates.

4.1.1 Complex Predicates

Light verb constructions are common in Sinhala; specifically, they can be found in noun-verb, adjective–verb and particle-verb constructions. There are two verbs that function as light verbs in Sinhala: කර *kara*, the volitive indicator and වෙ *ve*, the involitive indicator. Further, similar to most South Asian Languages, Sinhala also has verb-verb compounds, which involve collocations of two verbs (Slade and Aronoff, 2020). The other type of complex predicate in Sinhala is the phrasal verb, which is formed with nouns accompanied by verbs, except for the two light verbs mentioned above. For instance, පාඩම් කරයි *pāḍam karayi* study.non-past.3sg in Figure 6 is a CP in Sinhala with a light verb construction which has developed to a complex construction පාඩම් කර ගනියි *pāḍam kara ganiyi* get-studied.non-past.3sg in Figure 7.

Some UD treebanks such as Hindi (Tandon et al., 2016) and Punjabi (Arora, 2022) use the carrier of grammatical functions, which is the second token of the compound as the head of the complex predicates. However, we treated the first token or the semantic head of the complex predicate as the head of the relation, as used by Krishnamurthy and Sarveswaran (2021), since the second token only carries the grammatical functions.

Sinhala complex predicate constructions can be divided into three categories: i) Head + LVC[2], ii) Head + SVC[3], and iii) Head + Com[4]. To differentiate from the other two, the second element of category 3 was annotated as a compound. Table 4 lists the occurrences of all three constructions found in the treebank.

[2]Light Verb Construction

Aux	Function	Example
tibe	Aspct-perf	*dalvā tibe* have lit
æta	Aspct-perf	*dalvā æta* have lit
	Aspct-prosp	*dalvanu æta* will be lit
næta	Aspct-perf-neg	*dalvā næta* have not lit
siṭi	Aspct-prog	*dalvamin siṭi* {be}lighting
pavati	Aspct-prog	*dalvamin pavati* {be}lighting
yutu	Modal-nec	*dælviya yutu* should be lit
hæki	Modal-pot	*dælviya hæki* can be lit
laba	Pasv-NonPast	*dalvanu laba* light
lada	Pasv-Past	*dalvana lada* lit

Table 6: Auxiliaries in the Sinhala language.

4.1.2 Auxiliary Verbs

The auxiliaries in Sinhala can be treated for several functions. They include aspectual (Aspect), modal and passive (Pass) auxiliaries. Further, the roles of the aspectual auxiliaries can be perfect (perf), progressive (prog) or prospective (prosp), and that of modal auxiliaries be either necessitative (nec) or potential (pot). Moreover, two passive auxiliaries occur for past and non-past in Sinhala. Except ලද *lada*, the passive-past auxiliary, all the other auxiliaries occur in the treebank. Auxiliaries in the Sinhala language are exemplified in Table 6 using the verb stem දල්ව- *dalva* (light-up).

4.1.3 Non-verbal Predicates

According to Gair and Paolillo (1988), a wide range of sentences in Sinhala lacks overt verbal predication. As given in Table 5, the treebank consists of 33 sentences with non-verbal predicates.

[3]Serial Verb Construction
[4]Compound

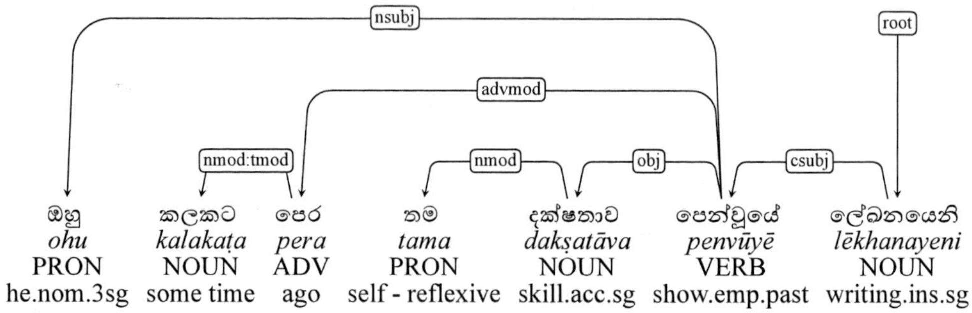

'It was through writing that he demonstrated his talent some time ago.'

Figure 1: Dependency relations in a focus construction

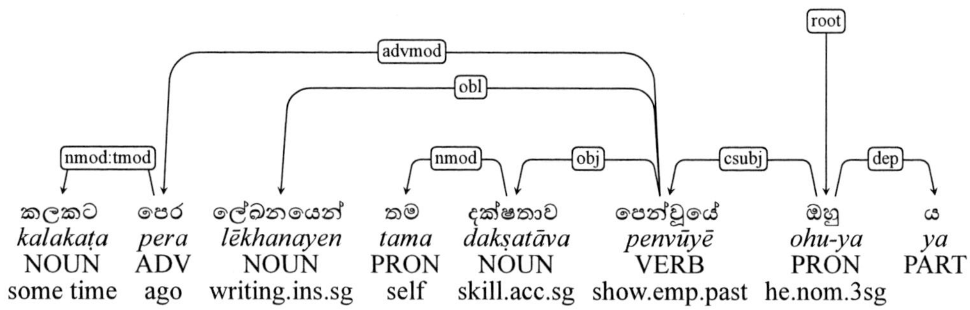

'It was he who demonstrated his talent in writing some time ago.'

Figure 2: Dependency relations with shifted emphasis for the sentence in Figure 1

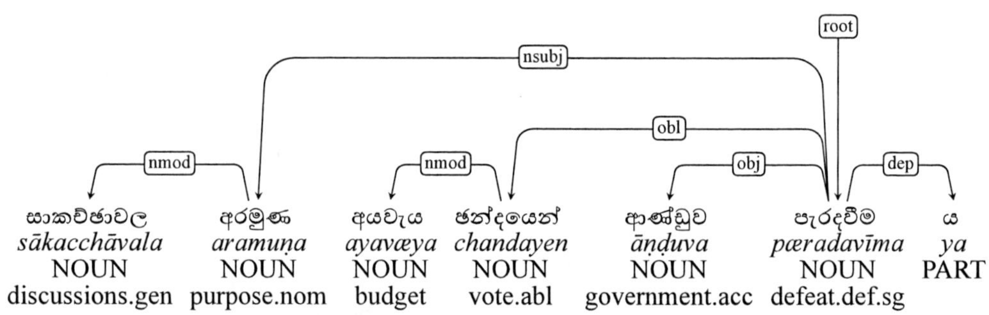

'The purpose of the discussions is to defeat the government in the budget vote.'

Figure 3: Dependency relations in a topic-comment construction

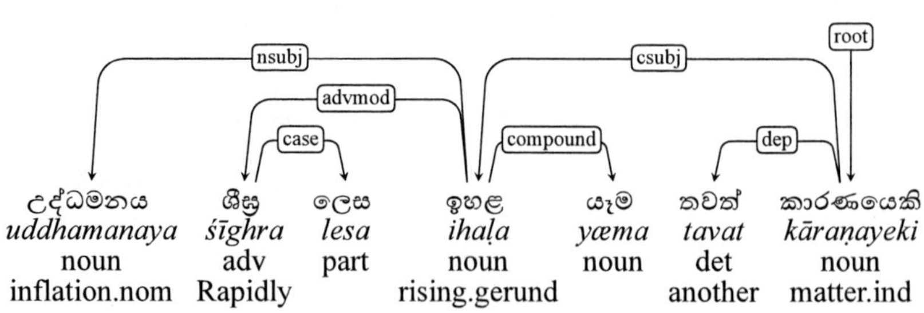

'Rapidly rising inflation is another matter.'

Figure 4: csubj in a topic-comment construction

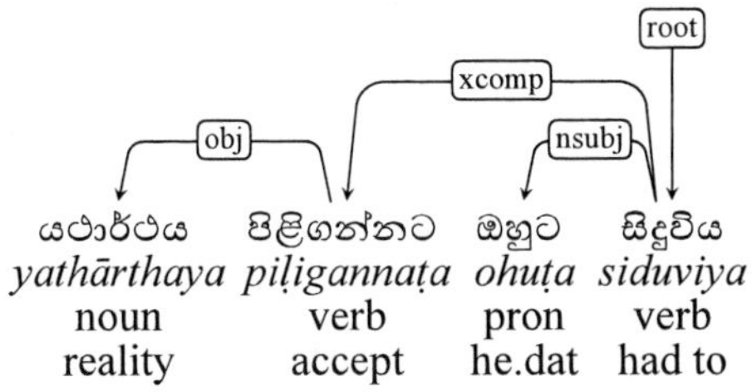

'He had to accept the reality'

Figure 5: A sentence with a clausal complement

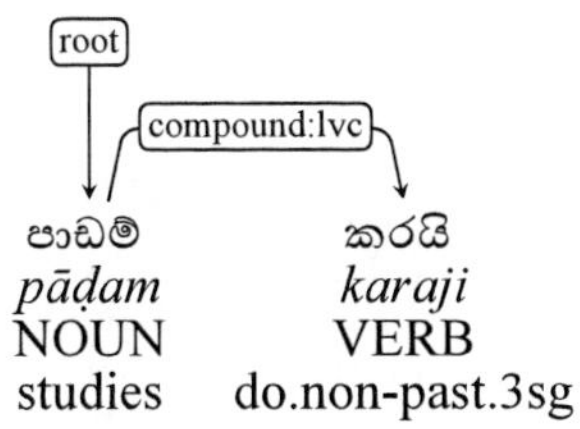

'study'

Figure 6: A Noun+LVC Construction

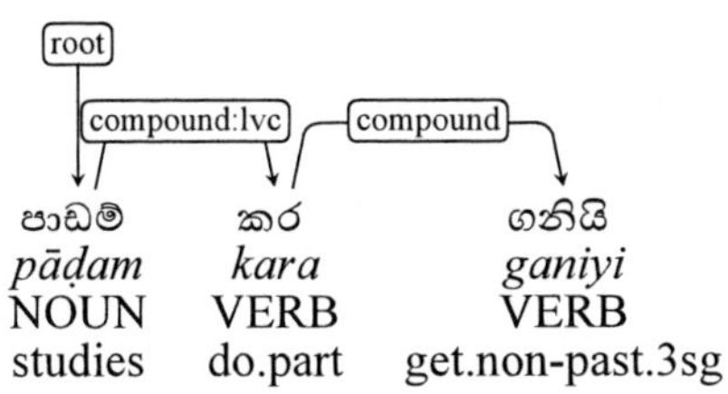

'get studied'

Figure 7: A Noun+LVC(compound) Construction

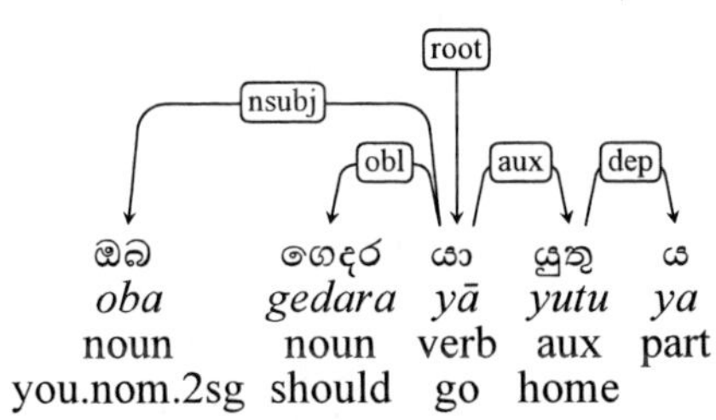

'You should go home'

Figure 8: A sentence with a modal auxiliary

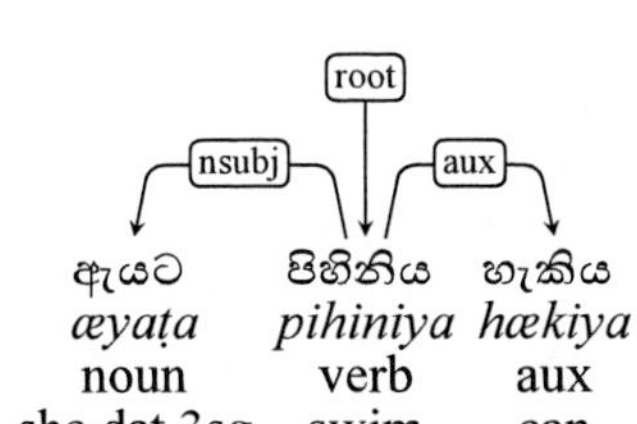

'She can swim'

Figure 9: A sentence with a dative subject

Sentences with non-verbal predicates can further be classified into the following three types based on their syntactic structure.

i. Focus Constructions: Gair and Sumangala (1991) and Slade (2011) state that there are several methods for creating focus constructions in Sinhala, one of which is the use of an emphatic form. The treebank contains numerous sentences employing this technique. Figure 1 displays a sentence where the focus is placed on a noun, which serves as the root of the sentence. The verb acts as the clausal subject and is the direct dependent of the root, with all other elements dependent on it. When a sentence is transformed into a focus construction, the main verb adopts an emphatic form (Gair and Paolillo, 1988). In the sentence of Figure 1 පෙන්ව- *penva*, the verb root has changed into the emphatic form පෙන්වූයේ *penvūyē* and has become the head of the clausal subject. The lexical item that is being focused on, which serves as the root of the sentence, is often followed by the emphatic form. Since Sinhala word order is relatively free, there are occasions where the emphasized lexical item may appear first. However, the emphatic form always depends on the emphasized lexical item. For instance, if the focus is placed on the lexical item ඔහු *ohu*, which serves as the nominal subject of the sentence in Figure 1, the sentence will transform into the sentence depicted in Figure 2, where ඔහු *ohu* is followed by an emphatic form.

ii. Copula Constructions: Sinhala is a language with zero copula; the only be verb වේ *ve:* or වෙයි *veji*, which have the same lexical root, comes in the copula position in literary Sinhala. Unlike in English, copula in Sinhala can be elided, which will not affect the syntactic structure. For instance, Figure 10 is a copula construction in Sinhala. The copula can be replaced with the sentence ending particle ය *ya* as an indication of the sentence ending. Further, Figure 11 shows a sentence with a null copula, but still, the sentence is a complete one. This particular construction is also in literary form. Interestingly, although there are no copula, a suffix 'i'[5] is used to mark the predication.

iii. Topic-Comment Constructions: In topic-comment constructions, the nominal subject depends on the nominal predicate, which is exemplified in Figure 3.

[5] 'i' marker is not discussed in the Sinhala literature. However, based on the analysis of several constructions, we concluded that 'i' marks the predication in this particular case. However, this requires more linguistic exploration.

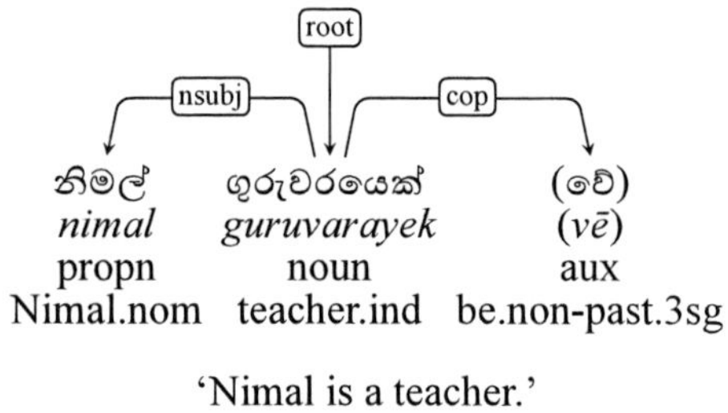

Figure 10: Copula construction

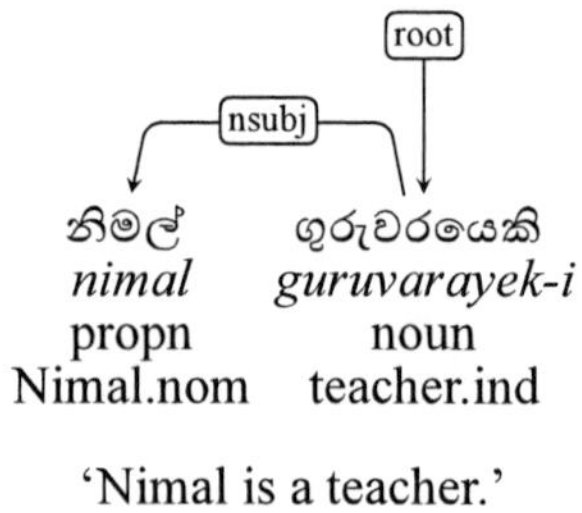

Figure 11: A zero copula construction

4.2 Core Arguments in Sinhala

As discussed in 4.1.3, nonverbal predicates are common in Sinhala; therefore, relatively more clausal subjects can be seen in the data. These clausal subjects predominantly occur in focus constructions compared to topic-comment constructions. For instance, Figure 1 is a focus construction and occurs `csubj`. However, both Figure 3 and Figure 4 are topic-comment constructions where Figure 4 consists of a `csubj` but not in Figure 3. Further, Figure 5 depicts a construction with `xcomp` along with a `nsubj`.

Sinhala also has non-canonical subjects with dative case marking which are referred to as dative subjects (Chandralal, 2010). According to Prasanna (2021) dative subjects can be found in a variety of sentence constructions, including involitive doers, possessive subjects, Abilitative Subjects, etc. Figure 9 illustrates the occurrence of dative subjects along with potential[6] modal verbs. In addition, dative subjects can occur in sentences with possessive verbs. Sinhala has two such possessive verbs: සිටි *siti* — with animate objects and තිබෙ *tibe* — with inanimate objects. The respective constructions are shown in Figure 12 and 13. Apart from functioning as possessive verbs, these two can also function as aspectual auxiliaries as given in Table 6.

[6]The term `potential` is borrowed from the Universal Dependencies annotation documentation - `https://universaldependencies.org/u/feat/all.html#Pot`

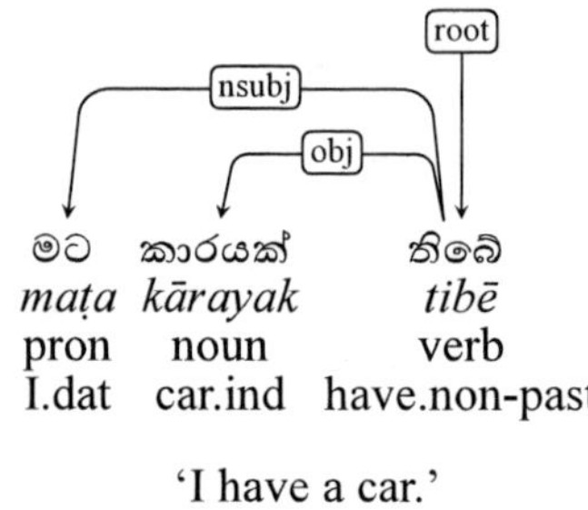

Figure 12: Dative subject with an inanimate object

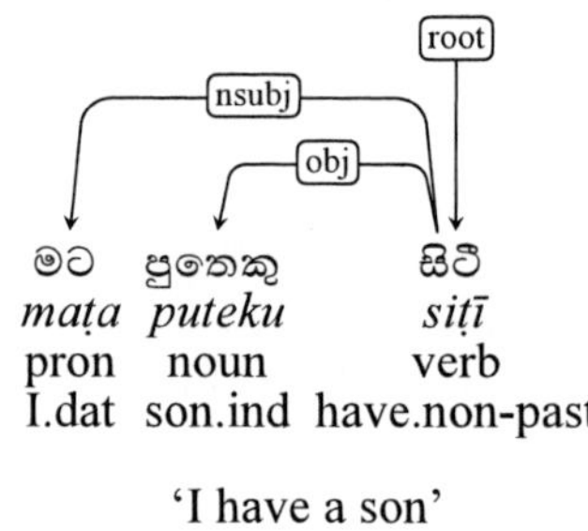

Figure 13: Dative subject with an animate object

5 Issues and Challenges

This section outlines some of the challenges we encountered during the linguistic analysis and annotation.

5.1 Lack of morphological feature labels

In Sinhala, ගුරුවරයෙකි *guruvarayek-i* and ගුරුවරයෙක් *guruvarayek* (teacher.Ind) refer to the same lexical element and can function as nonverbal predicates. The suffix '-i' that we have identified as the predicate marker cannot be marked with the existing features set available in the Universal Dependencies or UniMorph. Therefore, we introduced a new feature called `predicate` with the value 'yes'[7] to mark whether a word is a predicate or not.

5.2 Challenges with Dependency Annotation

The particle '*-ya*' in Literary Sinhala has been described as a predicative marker by Gair and Karuṇātilaka (1974); however, it can more accurately be identified as a sentence-ending marker. It is semantically empty but marks the end of the sentence, as shown in Figure 2 and Figure 3. When a predicate is accompanied by an auxiliary, the particle '*-ya*' can be written either together with the `AUX` or as a separate token following the `AUX`. As shown

[7]Here we followed the UD specification to define the feature `predicate` and the value 'yes'

in Figure 8 '*-ya*' that appears after the AUX must be marked as a dependent of the AUX. However, the Universal Dependencies (UD) schema does not allow auxiliaries to have children, so dependents of AUX are not permitted in the current UD specification.

6 Conclusion

We have reported the development of the first treebank for the Sinhala language, which is annotated using the Universal Dependencies framework. As a first attempt, we have annotated 100 sentences taken from a contemporary Sinhala text corpus. Apart from the data selection and the annotation process, we have also given analyses for the interesting constructions found in the data and explained how we had captured them using the current Universal Dependencies specification.

Acknowledgements

This research was made possible with the support of the UCSC research fund. The authors express their gratitude to Dr. Ruvan Weerasinghe, a senior lecturer at UCSC, for his support and encouragement in making this research successful. Authors also extend their appreciation to Prof. W.M. Wijeratne and Ms. Lakshika Madushani from the Department of Linguistics at the University of Kelaniya for their support. Lastly, the authors thank Mr. Vincent Halahakone for helping with the language corrections.

References

Aryaman Arora. 2022. Universal Dependencies for Punjabi. In *Proceedings of the Thirteenth Language Resources and Evaluation Conference*, pages 5705–5711.

Rafiya Begum, Samar Husain, Arun Dhwaj, Dipti Misra Sharma, Lakshmi Bai, and Rajeev Sangal. 2008. Dependency annotation scheme for Indian languages. In *Proceedings of the Third International Joint Conference on Natural Language Processing: Volume-II*.

Pushpak Bhattacharyya, Hema Murthy, Surangika Ranathunga, and Ranjiva Munasinghe. 2019. Indic language computing. *Communications of the ACM*, 62(11):70–75.

Dileep Chandralal. 2010. Sinhala. *Sinhala*, pages 1–312.

Nisansa de Silva. 2019. Survey on Publicly Available Sinhala Natural Language Processing Tools and Research. *arXiv preprint arXiv:1906.02358*.

EPD. 2014. *Sinhala lēkhana vyavahāraya - upadēśa samgrahaya*. Educational Publications Department, Sri Lanka.

Aloka Fernando, Surangika Ranathunga, Dilan Sachintha, Lakmali Piyarathna, and Charith Rajitha. 2022. Exploiting bilingual lexicons to improve multilingual embedding-based document and sentence alignment for low-resource languages. *Knowledge and Information Systems*.

James Gair and Lelwala Sumangala. 1991. What to focus in sinhala. In *The proceedings of the Eastern States Conference on Linguistics (ESCOL)*, volume 91, pages 93–108.

James W Gair. 1968. Sinhalese diglossia. *Anthropological Linguistics*, pages 1–15.

James W Gair and Ḍabliv Es Karuṇātilaka. 1974. *Literary Sinhala*. South Asia Program and Department of Modern Languages and Linguistics.

James W Gair and John C Paolillo. 1988. Sinhala nonverbal sentences and argument structure. *Cornell working papers in linguistics*, 8:39–77.

Francisco Guzmán, Peng-Jen Chen, Myle Ott, Juan Pino, Guillaume Lample, Philipp Koehn, Vishrav Chaudhary, and Marc'Aurelio Ranzato. 2019. The FLORES Evaluation Datasets for Low-Resource Machine Translation: Nepali–English and Sinhala–English. In *Proceedings of the 2019 Conference on Empirical Methods in Natural Language Processing and the 9th International Joint Conference on Natural Language Processing (EMNLP-IJCNLP)*, pages 6098–6111, Hong Kong, China. Association for Computational Linguistics.

Nizar Habash. 2007. Syntactic Preprocessing for Statistical Machine Translation. In *Proceedings of Machine Translation Summit XI: Papers*, pages 215–222, Copenhagen, Denmark. Association for Computational Linguistics.

WS Karunatillake. 2009. *Sinhala bhasha vyakaranaya*. M. D. Gunasena Co. Ltd, Sri Lanka.

Parameswari Krishnamurthy and Kengatharaiyer Sarveswaran. 2021. Towards Building a Modern Written Tamil Treebank. In *Proceedings of the 20th International Workshop on Treebanks and Linguistic Theories (TLT, SyntaxFest 2021)*, pages 61–68.

Junhui Li, Deyi Xiong, Zhaopeng Tu, Muhua Zhu, Min Zhang, and Guodong Zhou. 2017. Modeling Source Syntax for Neural Machine Translation. In *Proceedings of the 55th Annual Meeting of the Association for Computational Linguistics (Volume 1: Long Papers)*, pages 688–697, Vancouver, Canada. Association for Computational Linguistics.

Chamila Liyanage, Randil Pushpananda, Dulip Lakmal Herath, and Ruvan Weerasinghe. 2012. A computational grammar of Sinhala. In *International Conference on Intelligent Text Processing and Computational Linguistics*, pages 188–200. Springer.

Chamila Liyanage and WM Wijeratne. 2017. Developing a Dependency Tag Set for Sinhala: Procedure and Issues. In *Proceedings of Third International Conference on Linguistics in Sri Lanka (ICLSL 2017)*. Unviersity of Kelaniya, Sri Lanka.

Michael C McCord, J William Murdock, and Branimir K Boguraev. 2012. Deep Parsing in Watson. *IBM Journal of Research and Development*, 56(3.4):3–1.

NIE. 2015. *Sinhala lēkhana rītiya - New Edition*. National Institute of Education, Sri Lanka.

Tomoko Ohta, Yusuke Miyao, Takashi Ninomiya, Yoshimasa Tsuruoka, Akane Yakushiji, Katsuya Masuda, Jumpei Takeuchi, Kazuhiro Yoshida, Tadayoshi Hara, Jin-Dong Kim, et al. 2006. An intelligent search engine and GUI-based efficient MEDLINE search tool based on deep syntactic parsing. In *Proceedings of the COLING/ACL 2006 Interactive Presentation Sessions*, pages 17–20.

Warahena Liyanage Chamila Prasanna. 2021. *An Exploration of Dependency Grammar for Sinhala Language*. Unpublished MPhil thesis, University of Kelaniya.

Vinit Ravishankar. 2017. A Universal Dependencies treebank for Marathi. In *Proceedings of the 16th international workshop on treebanks and linguistic theories*, pages 190–200.

Benjamin Slade and Mark Aronoff. 2020. Verb Concatenation in Asian Linguistics. In *Oxford Research Encyclopedia of Linguistics*.

Benjamin Martin Slade. 2011. *Formal and philological inquiries into the nature of interrogatives, indefinites, disjunction, and focus in Sinhala and other languages*. University of Illinois at Urbana-Champaign.

Juhi Tandon, Himani Chaudhry, Riyaz Ahmad Bhat, and Dipti Misra Sharma. 2016. Conversion from Paninian karakas to Universal Dependencies for Hindi dependency treebank. In *Proceedings of the 10th Linguistic Annotation Workshop held in conjunction with ACL 2016 (LAW-X 2016)*, pages 141–150.

Junru Zhou, Zhuosheng Zhang, Hai Zhao, and Shuailiang Zhang. 2020. LIMIT-BERT : Linguistics Informed Multi-Task BERT. In *Findings of the Association for Computational Linguistics: EMNLP 2020*, pages 4450–4461, Online. Association for Computational Linguistics.

Methodological issues regarding the semi-automatic UD treebank creation of under-resourced languages: the case of Pomak

Stella Markantonatou Nicolaos Th. Constantinides Vivian Stamou
Vasileios Arampatzakis Panagiotis G. Krimpas George Pavlidis
Institute for Language and Speech Processing, Athena R.C.
{marks, n.konstantinidis, vistamou, vasilis.arampatzakis, p.krimpas, gpavlid}@athenarc.gr

Abstract

Pomak is an endangered oral Slavic language of Thrace/Greece. We present a short description of its interesting morphological and syntactic features in the UD framework. Because the morphological annotation of the treebank takes advantage of existing resources, it requires a different methodological approach from the one adopted for syntactic annotation that has started from scratch. It also requires the option of obtaining morphological predictions/evaluation separately from the syntactic ones with state-of-the-art NLP tools. Active annotation is applied in various settings in order to identify the best model that would facilitate the ongoing syntactic annotation.

1 Introduction

The development of the Pomak UD (Universal Dependencies) treebank was carried out as a case study of the project PHILOTIS, which aims at providing the infrastructure for the multimodal documentation of living languages.[1] Pomak is an endangered oral Slavic language of historical Thrace (South Balkans). Morphological and syntactic annotation are carried out in two distinct settings because the first one uses existing resources and the second one starts from scratch.

Sections 2 and 3 briefly present the current situation of Pomak language, the script/orthography adopted for the development of its treebank and the available resources. In Section 4 a short linguistic description of Pomak is given in the UD framework. The annotation procedure is discussed in Section 5. Conclusions and future plans are presented in Section 6.

2 About Pomak

Pomak (endonym: Pomácky, Pomácko, Pomácku or other dialectal variants) is a non-standardised East South Slavic language variety.[2] Pomak is spoken in Bulgaria and Greece (mainly in the Rhodope Mountain area), in the European part of Turkey and in places of Pomak diaspora (Constantinides 2007: 35). The Pomak dialect continuum has been influenced by Greek and Turkish due to extensive bilingualism or trilingualism (Adamou and Fanciullo, 2018).

Pomak scores low on all six factors of language vitality and endangerment proposed by UNESCO (for more details see Brenzinger et al. 2003). In short, there is little written legacy of merely symbolic significance for the speakers of Pomak, the language is not taught at school, it is mainly used in family settings, which are increasingly penetrated by the dominant language(s) (Greek, Turkish).

Furthermore, Pomak showcases certain issues involved in the development of NLP resources for an oral, non-standardised language with some legacy such as texts and/or lexica of some type; this is the case for a number of, European at least, language varieties (Gerstenberger et al., 2017; Bernhard et al., 2021). The exploitation of the linguistic knowledge contained in such legacy may require (i) the transcription/transformation of the textual sources to the right processable format (ii) some adaptation of the processing pipelines offered by open-source state-of-the-art NLP tools. Both types of action were required for the development of the Pomak UD treebank.

3 Pomak textual sources and scripts

There are sporadic transcriptions and recordings of Pomak folk songs and tales as well as very few modern texts (mostly journalistic texts and translations from Greek and English into Pomak). The existing texts are written in a variety of scripts, ranging from Bulgarian-based Cyrillic to Modern Greek to an English-based Latin alphabet. PHILO-

[1] `https://philotis.athenarc.gr/`

[2] `https://elen.ngo/languages-map/`

Proceedings of the Sixth Workshop on Universal Dependencies (UDW, GURT/SyntaxFest 2023), pages 27 - 35
March 9-12, 2023 ©2023 Association for Computational Linguistics

TIS collected these scattered resources through a network of native speakers and Greek scholars who, for various reasons, are close to the Pomak community. Selected parts of this material are included in a corpus of about 130,000 words. The corpus will be made available on the web to institutions and individuals for research and innovation purposes; at the moment, it is available for the same purposes after personal contact with the first and/or last author. Table 1 shows the text genres included in the corpus and the size of the respective texts in words. Where possible, the geographical origin of the texts is also given as a hint to the dialect used in the text.

Text types	**Words**	**Geographical origins**
Folk tales	43.817	Emonio, Glafki, Dimario, Echinos, Myki, Pachni, Oreo
Language description	19.524	mixed
Journalism	25.236	Myki
Translations into Pomak	24.208	Myki, Pachni
Folk songs	18.434	mixed
Proverbs	550	mixed
Other	5.325	Myki

Table 1: Pomak corpus: type, size and geographical origins of texts.

We took advantage of the Pomak electronic lexicon Rodopsky, which contains about 61.500 lemmas corresponding to about 3.5 x 10^6 unique forms (i.e., combinations of a lexical token and a PoS symbol) annotated for lemma, PoS and morphological features.[3] Rodopsky, the existing textual sources and the fact that Pomak is a Slavic language have helped us solve several issues regarding Pomak orthography, namely identification of words and their grammatical function and the identification of inflectional paradigms. Still, a lot of work was required to adapt the linguistic information in Rodopsky and the textual legacy of Pomak to contemporary linguistics and UDs.

Text homogenisation work was necessary because Pomak texts, including Rodopsky, employ various orthographies. The Latin-based alphabet proposed by Ritvan Karahoǧa and Panagiotis G. Krimpas (hereinafter: K&K alphabet), which has a language resource-oriented accented version and a non-accented all-purpose version, was used to semi-automatically transliterate Rodopsky and the corpus. The K&K alphabet has been developed along the following lines (Karahóǧa et al., 2022): (i) Portability of the alphabet (use of UNICODE) (ii) Phonetic transparency (iii) Easily learned representations of sounds due to the use of similar diacritics for same articulation sounds and the absence of digraphs (iv) Consistent spelling not affected by predictable allophony; for instance, the de-voicing of b [b], d [d], g [g] in word-final position or before a voiceless consonant is not shown for the sake of consistency across the declension/conjugation paradigm, which is why *hlæb* 'bread (Nom|Sg)' is spelled with a b although it is actually pronounced [hlɛɐp] in order to ensure consistency across the clitic paradigm *hlæbu* 'of/to (the) bread', *hlæbove* 'breads (Nom|Pl)' etc. (v) The K&K alphabet is based on the dialect of Myki but it can also partially serve as a hyperdialectal script by allowing various predictable pronunciations of the same graph according to dialect; for instance, the vowel in the first syllable of *zømom* '(that) I take,' which is pronounced as [ø] in Myki, can also be acceptably pronounced as [jo] in Echinos or as [e] in Dimario, no matter that all three variants are spelled with an ø. This is because speakers from Echinos and Dimario have no [ø]-sound, which is why they spontaneously replace it with [jo] or [e], respectively, while speakers from Myki, if asked to read out the digraph jo or the graph e would not automatically pronounce them as [ø], given that they do have words with [jo] and [e] in their native variety. However, a hyperdialectal Pomak orthography is often not possible, given that some varieties differ also in the lexical and/or morphological level.

4 Pomak morphosyntax at a glance

A short morphosyntactic description of Pomak follows in the framework of Universal Dependencies, Version 2 (UD).[4]

4.1 Morphology of Pomak

In the orthography adopted, words are delimited by white space characters. Distributional and phonological criteria were applied regarding the place-

[3]https://www.rodopsky.gr/

[4]https://universaldependencies.org/treebanks/qpm_philotis/index.html

ment of white spaces with certain interrogative, indefinite and negative pronouns, conjunctions and adverbs that are spelled as a single word in most Slavic languages but as two words in the adopted Pomak orthography, e.g., *at kak* for *atkák* 'since', *ní kutrí* for *níkutrí* 'nobody' and *nó kadé* for *nókade* 'somewhere'. In all these cases, the first word can be independently identified as a preposition or particle, e.g., *at* 'from; out of', *kak* 'how; as; like', *kadé* 'where' and the second as an interrogative pronoun or adverb. The particles are assigned the PoS tag 'PART' and the feature 'PartTypeQpm' with one of the values 'Ind' (indefinite), 'Neg' (negative), 'Tot' (total). 'PartTypeQpm' is defined for Pomak.

In the general description of Pomak morphological features given below, certain interesting or very special cases are highlighted. The Pomak treebank uses 16 universal POS categories ('SYM' is not used).

4.1.1 The grammatical features gender, number, case and animacy

Pomak common and proper nouns, determiners, adjectives, pronouns, participles and some of the numerals are morphologically marked for gender, number, case and animacy (see below).

Gender, Case: Pomak overtly marks three genders (masculine, feminine, neuter) and four cases (nominative, genitive, accusative and vocative).

Animacy: The opposition 'Human vs. Nonhuman' is overt with masculine plural and rarely with masculine singular of adjectives, pronouns and participles.

Number: In addition to singular and plural number, Pomak also has:
(i) plurale tantum, e.g., *pantóly* 'pants', *diláve* 'fire tongs', *nallamý* 'pincers', collective nouns ending in *-ja* are always plural (the feature has not yet been implemented in the UD treebank)
(ii) count plural, used with masculine nouns after numerals; etymologically, this is a relic of the dual form, e.g. *dva balóna* 'two ballons', *dva kámenæ* 'two stones'
(iii) collective/mass/singulare tantum; collective nouns ending in *-(j)e*, despite having always plural (collective) meaning, can be either grammatically singular (a less frequent case) or grammatically plural, depending on the speaker's perception of the set of objects as a whole or as distinct items (dialectal variation is possible), e.g., *balóṇe / baloṇá* 'multitude of ballons".

With possessive determiners both the number of the possessor and the possessed object are encoded.

4.1.2 Diminutives; the tripartite enclitic definite article

Like most Balkan/Slavic languages, Pomak has a rich inventory of diminutive and augmentative forms of nouns, adjectives, adverbs and certain passive participles; the feature has been implemented in the UD treebank.

Pomak is special in that it uses a **tripartite enclitic definite article** *-s, -t, -n* (Adamou and Fanciullo, 2018; Krimpas, 2020) that occurs with nouns, adjectives, strong types of pronouns, certain numerals, adverbs and passive participles and denotes deixis and definiteness as follows:
(i) Proximity to the speaker, annotated as 'Deixis=Prox' and 'DeixisRef=1', e.g., *čulǽkos* 'the man close to the speaker'
(ii) Proximity to the listener, annotated as 'Deixis=Prox' and 'DeixisRef=2', e.g., *čulǽkot* 'the man close to the listener'
(iii) Distance from both the speaker and the listener, annotated as 'Deixis=Remt', e.g., *čulǽkon* 'the man who is away from both the speaker and the listener'.

The feature 'DeixisRef' has been defined for Pomak because the attested opposition between "proximity to the speaker" and "proximity to the listener" could not be modelled with the values available in UD for the feature 'Deixis' that do not distinguish among reference points.

4.1.3 Auxiliaries

The auxiliary *som* 'to be' is used to form perfect verb tenses and the passive voice. *som* is considered a verb (and bears the dependency relation 'root') when it means 'to exist' (1), or heads an impersonal clause with a phrasal subject (2).

(1) je górmon ad pó naprḗš itám
is forest from more near there
'A forest is nearby.'

(2) tébe tí je jálnis
you to you is only
da rečḗš krívo
to speak wickedly
'All you can do is to speak wickedly'

šom/štom and *še/ša* express possibility and, like the Greek θα, precede indicative verb forms to form the tense 'Future' (3).

(3) ja še tí dam halvá
I will you give halva
'I will give you halva (a kind of a candy)'

The question particle *li*, e.g., *dojdéš li* 'do you come?', is assigned the PoS label 'PART' and the dependency 'aux:q'.

4.1.4 Verbs

Modal verbs, personal and impersonal verbs, participles, infinitives and converbs are assigned the PoS 'VERB'.

Verbs have finite and non-finite forms. *Finite verbs* are marked for 'Mood' with values 'Ind' (indicative) or 'Imp' (imperative), one of the four values of 'Number' (see above) and one of the three values of 'Person': '1', '2' or '3'. Verbs in the 'Ind' mood are marked for one of the two values of 'Tense', namely 'Past' or 'Pres' (present).

As in all Slavic languages, *aspect* is either a lexical or a morphological feature of the verb; it is described with the values 'Imp'(imperfective) or 'Perf'(perfective) of the feature 'Aspect', e.g., *kázavom, kážom* 'to say/to narrate' respectively.

There are three types of *nonfinite verb forms*: converbs, participles and infinitives. Only passive participles are assigned the pair 'Voice=Pass'; all other verb forms are assigned the pair 'Voice=Act'.

The infinitive forms the prohibitive imperative (4) when it appears after the particles *na/ne* and *namój* (sing.)/*namójte* (pl.) 'not'.

(4) namój barzá
not you rush
'do not rush'

Interestingly, Pomak has another, innovative form of infinitive, which may be called the **morphologically reduplicated infinitive** ending in *-titi*, crystallised in a small number of imperfective verbs that are repeated as bilects denoting the continuous/monotonous/rythmic repetition of a motion,'e.g. *čúktiti čúktiti* 'hit and hit'.

To summarise, Pomak uses the UD morphological apparatus extensively, including features for diminutives, and defines two new Pomak-specific features, namely 'PartTypeQpm' and 'DeixisRef'.

4.2 Syntax of Pomak

The Pomak treebank implements most UD dependency relations (hereinafter: "dependencies"). So far, not used dependencies include: 'cop' (copula), and 'dep' (unspecified dependency). As syntactic annotation of Pomak is still ongoing, modifications may occur in future editions of the treebank. The introduction of the following two dependencies is among our plans: (i) 'cop', as in the standing edition of the Pomak treebank auxiliaries depend on content words with the dependency 'aux' for reasons of uniformity and, (ii) 'compound:lvc' (light verb construction).

4.2.1 Pomak: a nominative-accusative language

Subjects (dependency 'nsubj') are typically marked with the nominative case and objects (dependency 'obj') with the accusative, although some verbs select objects in the genitive case. Indirect objects ('iobj') are marked with the genitive/dative case, which is morphologically based on the Slavic dative case. Ethic datives are tagged with the dependency 'obl', e.g., **dečómne** *drago* ... 'the children like to ...'.

When the strong and the weak type of the personal pronoun cooccur, the strong type is assigned the dependency 'obl' (oblique) and the weak type the dependency 'expl' (expletive) (Figure 1).

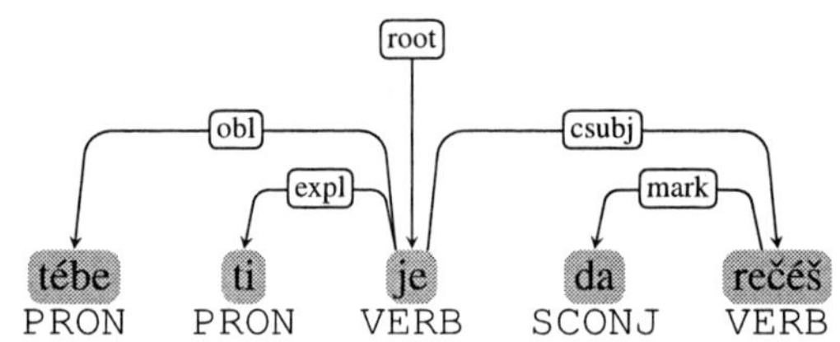

Figure 1: **tébe' ti** *je da rečéš* (literally: you to.you is to speak) 'it is up to you to speak'

The dependency 'expl:pass' is reserved for reflexive pronouns attached to transitive verbs as voice markers. Finally, the dependency 'expl:pv' is reserved for reflexive pronouns (*so, sa, se, si, su*) attached to verbs used as reflexives. In Pomak the dependency occurs with intransitive and certain transitive verbs (5).

(5) kopélkata **si** mýje rakýne
girl-the herself washes hands-the
'the girl washes her hands'

The dependency 'expl:impers' (expletive impersonal) is reserved for the reflexive pronoun (*só, sí, sé*) in impersonal constructions.

4.2.2 Compounds and fixed phrases

The dependency 'compound:redup' (reduplicated compounds) is used between pairs of identical words; in (6) reduplication serves emphasis purposes.

(6) adín sítan sítan dožd letǽšo
a soft soft rain was raining
'a very soft rain was falling'

The dependency 'fixed' essentially assigns a flat structure to fixed (multiword) expressions that behave like function words or short adverbials (Figure 2, Figure 3).

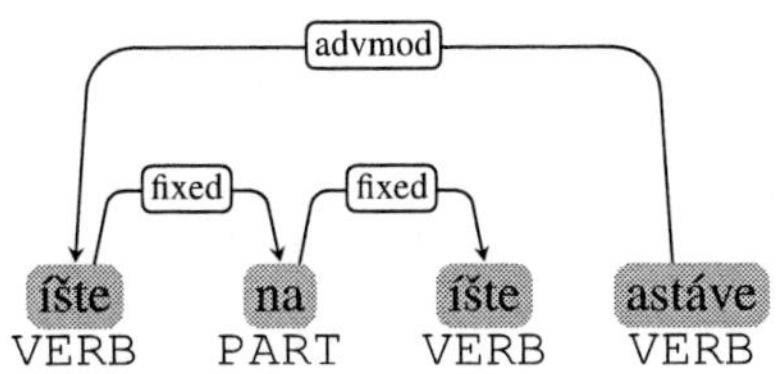

Figure 2: **íšte na íšte** *astáve gi faf kavenǿno* (literally: willing or not willing leaves them at café-the) 'willy-nilly he leaves them at the café'

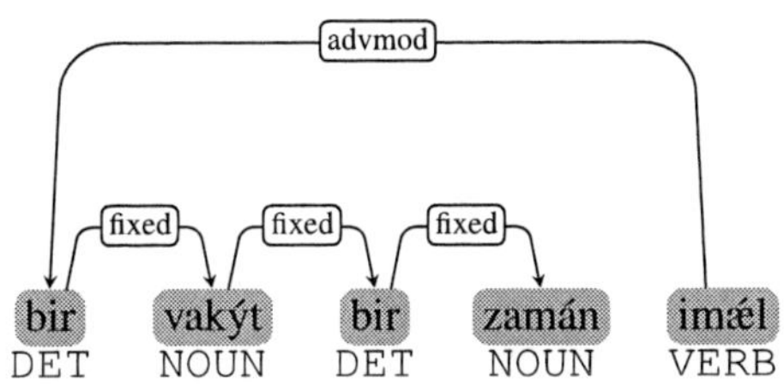

Figure 3: **bir vakýt bir zamán** *imǽl je adín čülǽk* (literally: one time one era has been a man) 'once upon a time there was a man'

Summing up, Pomak uses the UD syntactic apparatus extensively and so far, no new dependencies have been defined.

5 Development of the Pomak treebank

The UD Pomak treebank is developed in two distinct steps: morphological annotation and syntactic annotation. Different methodologies have been adopted for each step because background knowledge about Pomak morphology was available (in Rodopsky) while the description of Pomak syntax is an ongoing process intertwined with the annotation of the Pomak corpus with UD syntactic dependencies. Naturally, morphological annotation preceded syntactic annotation so the two steps are discussed below in this order.

5.1 Morphological annotation

Rodopsky was transcribed into the K&K orthography, the CONLLU format was adopted and the original morphological annotation was mapped semi-automatically on the UD framework by one native speaker and two linguists, one of them expert in UDs and the other in Slavic languages and Pomak. The transcribed and annotated Rodopsky was mapped on 6350 sentences (86,700 words) selected from the Pomak corpus to form the gold annotated corpus. Although in the case of endangered languages often there is a shortage of annotators, we were able to employ a native speaker and a Greek linguist fluent in Pomak who edited the corpus with very good interannotation agreement kappa scores on 476 sentences (PoS tags 0.90, features 0.87, lemmas 0.93) (Karahóğa et al., 2022). The gold corpus (hereinafter: 'QPMcorpus') has been uploaded on the UD language repository and included in the UD treebanks on which the recent edition of the Stanza tool has been trained.[5]

The procedure of assigning morphological annotation to the Pomak gold corpus was designed to exploit the resource Rodopsky. Although non standardised/oral languages and dialects may not be endowed with such legacy, when it exists, it is valuable and should be exploited; in fact, several European non-standardised languages have some textual legacy (Gerstenberger et al., 2017; Bernhard et al., 2021). In the merits of the selected approach are (i) the development of the morphologically annotated gold corpus proceeded faster because the annotators only edited good quality morphological tags (ii) the use of dedicated resources mitigated the effect of imposing knowledge from other languages onto the documented one through shared training language models (Bird, 2022) (see also the discussion on syntactic annotation) (iii) it made room for the active participation of the community in the documentation process of their native language. On the processing front, the existence of an independently created relatively substantial morphologically annotated gold corpus allowed us to test various open-source NLP tools, namely

[5] https://github.com/stanfordnlp/stanza/blob/main/stanza/models/common/constant.py

spaCy v3.2.2[6] (Honnibal et al., 2020), Stanza[7] (Qi et al., 2020), UDify[8] (Kondratyuk and Straka, 2019) and UDPipe[9] (Straka et al., 2016) (for details see (Karahóğa et al., 2022)) and select Stanza for its accuracy results in order to annotate our Pomak corpora.

A comment is due here: Like many open-source NLP tools (Nguyen et al., 2021), Stanza did not allow for the independent assignment and evaluation of morphological and syntactic annotation. Thus, an incremental corpus creation (active annotation) was not properly supported. Working with an unstudied language, like Pomak, in a project that targeted active corpus building, revealed that the morphological and syntactic annotation processes should be independent. Thus, we manipulated the Stanza code in order to separate the two annotation processes. We also reported the issue to the Stanza development team and, as a result, the updated Stanza version provides an approach for the required separate annotations.[10]

5.2 Syntactic annotation

In this section we describe the ongoing syntactic annotation of the QPMcorpus that will eventually yield the Pomak morphologically and syntactically annotated gold corpus (Pomak UD treebank).

5.2.1 Data, tools and methods

Drawing on our experience from morphological annotation, we use Stanza to support the syntactic annotation of the QPMcorpus. We have adopted the active annotation method (Settles, 2009; Anastasopoulos et al., 2018; Shi et al., 2021) because, contrary to Pomak morphology, there is no prior 'formal' approach to Pomak syntax. As a result, a formal description of the syntactic properties of Pomak is developed as the annotation of parts of the QPMcorpus advances. Active annotation, as it is shown schematically in Figure 4, unfolds in cycles where an initial model is trained on an available dataset, it is then applied on unseen data, its output is edited manually, the data on which the model is re-trained include the original material and the edited one and so on. This procedure only partially corresponds to the actual annotation procedure of a language for which prior knowledge is not available. This is because at each annotation cycle, the annotators' knowledge about the language increases and, possibly, the annotation guidelines are modified enforcing the editing of all the material used so far to train the model (and not only of the output of the previous cycle). We still hope that active annotation will minimize annotation workload but we intend to study this issue more systematically in the immediate future with more annotation cycles. Annotation is performed by a Greek linguist fluent in Pomak who is advised by native speakers, an expert in Slavic languages and Pomak and a computational linguist familiar with the UD framework. As opposed to morphology, in the case of syntactic annotation we were not able to employ more than one expert mainly because there were no background extensive studies of Pomak syntax.

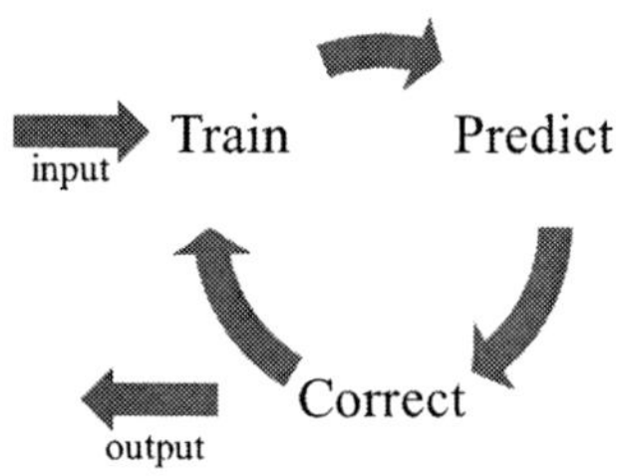

Figure 4: The active annotation procedure.

To better understand the effect of pre-existing knowledge from languages similar to Pomak on the model's performance, we created two corpora: (i) the "sl+po" corpus, comprising the QPMcorpus and annotated text retrieved from the UD treebanks of other languages in the South Slavic language group to which Pomak belongs, namely Bulgarian, Croatian, Serbian, and Slovene plus Slovac which is a West Slavic language whose alphabet is very similar to the Pomak one; treebanks in Cyrillic scripts were transliterated into Latin script with UROMAN[11] (ii) the "bg+po" corpus, consisting of the Bulgarian UD treebank only.[12] In order to have a more balanced dataset in terms of size, we copied the available syntactically annotated Pomak sentences as many times as needed to reach the same order of magnitude, namely about 4000 sentences.

In addition, we created word embeddings with the "sl+po" corpus, which is a superset of the

[6]https://spacy.io/.
[7]https://stanfordnlp.github.io/stanza/.
[8]https://github.com/Hyperparticle/udify.
[9]https://ufal.mff.cuni.cz/udpipe/1/models
[10]https://stanfordnlp.github.io/stanza/new_language.html.
[11]https://github.com/isi-nlp/uroman.
[12]https://universaldependencies.org/

"bg+po" corpus. We used UROMAN to transliterate into Latin those treebanks that employ scripts based on the Cyrillic alphabet.[13] With the fasttext2 tool (skipgram method) set to default parameters we created 16738 x 100 word embeddings. The 16738 words originate in the mixture of the "sl+po" and the original Pomak corpus (130000 words) from which the QPMcorpus was extracted.

5.2.2 Experiments

We followed two lines of experimentation:
1. *Train all processors* for both morphology and syntax, resulting in the following three models:

- base (only Pomak)
- bg + po (Bulgarian + Pomak)
- sl + po (5 Slavic languages + Pomak)

2. *Train for syntax only*; we loaded our best morphological model (indicated with the label "gm") that was trained on the QPMcorpus[14] (Karahóğa et al., 2022). Results of this process were the following three models:

- base-gm (only Pomak)
- bg + po-gm (Bulgarian + Pomak)
- sl + po-gm (Slavic + Pomak)

Each training used a typical 80%—10%—10% data split for the training, validation and testing sets. In Table 2, the labels "**a**" and "**b**" indicate the manually annotated Pomak corpora used for the first and second active annotation cycles respectively. We report on the following metrics: Unlabeled Attachment Score (UAS), Labeled Attachment Score (LAS), Content-word Labeled Attachment Score (CLAS), Morphology-aware Labeled Attachment Score (MLAS) and Bi-LExical dependency Score (BLEX) (Zeman et al., 2018).

	Corpus	Train	Dev	Test
Sentences	**a**	184	16	16
Tokens		2033	178	208
Sentences	**b**	342	42	42
Tokens		3956	489	546

Table 2: Manually annotated Pomak corpora used in the two active annotation cycles.

We set as a baseline the UPOS, UAS and LAS values obtained with the first cycle of training on corpus **a** only, as reported in the first line of Table 3. In the second cycle we did not use the "sl+po" corpus, because in the first cycle it resulted in lower metric scores than those attained by the "bg" corpus (see Table 3). The results of the "sl" model suggest that it may be better to rely on models of few, or even one, very similar languages than models obtained from a branch of languages (including the branch to which the studied language belongs). However, our results do not suggest that Bulgarian is the language most similar to Pomak among the East South Slavic languages because we have not experimented with each one of the remaining languages in the "sl" model. Another reason for avoiding training on the "sl+po" corpus was the considerably long processing time required, due to its large size.

Model	UPOS (%)	UAS (%)	LAS (%)
base	84.62	73.56	58.65
base-gm	97.12	77.88	63.46
sl+po	87.50	75.48	64.42
sl+po-gm	97.12	79.81	68.27
bg+po	83.65	76.44	60.10
bg+po-gm	97.12	**82.69**	**69.23**

Table 3: UPOS, UAS, and LAS obtained with models trained and tested on corpus **a**.

The results of the two annotation cycles are summarised in Table 4 (in %), where boldface numbers denote the best model per task and per cycle. These results were obtained with a test set of 42 annotated sentences (extracted from corpus **b**).

Two annotation cycles with the same guidelines do not provide enough evidence for reliable conclusions. However, some interesting observations can be made:
1. Impact of gold morphology (model "gm") on metrics: syntactic predictions were improved considerably in all settings. This result supports our choice to exploit the resource Rodopsky and propose the modification of the process pipelines offered by the NLP tools.
2. Impact of increasing amounts of manually annotated data at the second annotation cycle (indicated with the "b" subscript):
2.1. As expected, the metrics of the models obtained from manually annotated Pomak data only (base_a, base_b) are improved as the annotated data increase in size (Anastasopoulos et al., 2018). However, one may notice that the best results in cycle **b**

[13]`https://github.com/isi-nlp/uroman.`

[14]In this approach, we attained a UD Part of Speech tags (UPOS) accuracy of 98.73% and a UD morphological features (UFEATS) accuracy of 95.23%.

Model	UPOS	UFeats	AllTags	Lemmas	UAS	LAS	CLAS	MLAS	BLEX
base_a	86.81	73.08	69.96	81.50	75.64	62.45	54.83	32.07	37.93
base-gm_a	98.72	98.35	97.25	99.27	83.70	71.61	65.07	59.59	64.73
sl+po_a	89.74	75.09	68.32	70.51	79.12	69.96	64.24	38.19	43.06
sl+po-gm_a	98.72	98.35	97.25	99.27	84.43	74.18	67.79	62.08	67.45
bg+po_a	85.53	71.98	67.77	80.59	73.99	61.72	53.04	30.41	39.86
bg+po-gm_a	**98.72**	**98.35**	**97.25**	**99.27**	**88.28**	**79.67**	**73.29**	**69.18**	**72.95**
base_b	91.03	81.50	78.57	86.63	81.50	70.88	62.80	45.39	51.19
base-gm_b	98.72	98.35	97.25	99.27	84.80	75.27	67.59	63.10	67.24
bg+po_b	91.58	84.25	80.40	86.26	82.05	71.61	66.43	47.20	55.59
bg+po-gm_b	**98.72**	**98.35**	**97.25**	**99.27**	**86.63**	**76.92**	**72.57**	**66.67**	**72.22**

Table 4: Metrics (%) of the two cycles (corpora **a** and **b**) obtained with the same test set, namely 42 sentences extracted from corpus b.

are a bit lower than those of cycle **a**, which seems counter-intuitive. It is our understanding that this is due to the instability of the learning process at the initial cycles, which deal with a limited number of samples (sentences) available for training. Nevertheless, the results are indicative and are expected to stabilize and improve in the next annotation cycles.

2.2. The difference between the scores obtained with models base-gm_b and bg+po-gm_b (for instance, for the UAS metric: 86.63%-84.80%=1.83%) is less than the respective difference between base-gm_a and bg+po-gm_a (for the UAS metric: 88.27%-83.70%=4.57%). This may be an encouraging development because it suggests that a point will be reached where a supportive language (here, Bulgarian) will not be necessary in few additional annotation cycles.

6 Discussion and Future work

We have presented the procedure we adopted to develop a UD treebank of Pomak, an endangered oral language of the East South Slavic group. The task is a case study of the project PHILOTIS and was supported by a group of computational linguists, linguists fluent in Slavic languages and Pomak and engineers as well as by the Pomak community.

Pomak exploited the UD inventory of labels and exposed unique linguistic phenomena regarding the system of Deixis and the verb system; modelling of Deixis led to the definition of a new UD morphological feature.

In this work we had the opportunity to apply two different annotation methods, one exploiting background knowledge (morphology) and one developing knowledge from scratch. The exploitation of background knowledge led to excellent accuracy scores with minimal annotation effort, however, few languages are endowed with the required resources. Therefore, an evaluation of the active annotation method that assumes no previous (morphological and/or syntactic) knowledge may be of more general interest. As the syntactic annotation of Pomak is still going on, a better understanding of the method, e.g., its impact on annotation time and costs, is among our immediate plans.

Acknowledgements

We acknowledge support of this work by the project "PHILOTIS: State-of-the-art technologies for the recording, analysis and documentation of living languages" (MIS 5047429), which is implemented under the "Action for the Support of Regional Excellence", funded by the Operational Programme "Competitiveness, Entrepreneurship and Innovation" (NSRF 2014-2020) and co-financed by Greece and the European Union (European Regional Development Fund).

References

Evangelia Adamou and Davide Fanciullo. 2018. Why Pomak will not be the next Slavic literary language. In D. Stern, M. Nomachi, and B. Belić, editors, *Linguistic regionalism in Eastern Europe and beyond: minority, regional and literary microlanguages*, pages 40–65. Peter Lang.

Antonios Anastasopoulos, Marika Lekakou, Josep Quer, Eleni Zimianiti, Justin DeBenedetto, and David Chiang. 2018. Part-of-speech tagging on an endangered language: a parallel Griko-Italian resource. In *Proceedings of the 27th International Conference on Computational Linguistics*, pages 2529–2539, Santa

Fe, New Mexico, USA. Association for Computational Linguistics.

Delphine Bernhard, Anne-Laure Ligozat, Myriam Bras, Fanny Martin, Marianne Vergez-Couret, Pascale Erhart, Jean Sibille, Amalia Todirascu, Philippe Boula de Mareüil, and Dominique Huck. 2021. Collecting and annotating corpora for three under-resourced languages of France: Methodological issues. *Language Documentation & Conservation*, 15:316–357.

Steven Bird. 2022. Local languages, third spaces, and other high-resource scenarios. In *Proceedings of the 60th Annual Meeting of the Association for Computational Linguistics (Volume 1: Long Papers)*, pages 7817–7829, Dublin, Ireland. Association for Computational Linguistics.

Matthias Brenzinger, Akira Yamamoto, Noriko Aikawa, Dmitri Koundiouba, Anahit Minasyan, Arienne Dwyer, Colette Grinevald, Michael Krauss, Osahito Miyaoka, Osamu Sakiyama, et al. 2003. Language vitality and endangerment. *Paris: UNESCO Intangible Cultural Unit, Safeguarding Endangered Languages.*

Nicolaos Th. Constantinides. 2007. *Units of the Pomak civilization in Greek Thrace. Brief historical review,language and identities.* Democritus University of Thrace:MA Thesis.

Ciprian-Virgil Gerstenberger, Niko Partanen, and Michael Rießler. 2017. Instant annotations in ELAN corpora of spoken and written Komi, an endangered language of the Barents Sea region. In *Proceedings of the 2nd Workshop on the Use of Computational Methods in the Study of Endangered Languages, Honolulu, Hawai*, pages 57–66.

Matthew Honnibal, Ines Montani, Sofie Van Landeghem, and Adriane Boyd. 2020. spaCy: Industrial-strength Natural Language Processing in Python.

Ritván Jusúf Karahóğa, Panagiotis G Krimpas G., Vivian Stamou, Vasileios Arampatzakis, Dimitrios Karamatskos, Vasileios Sevetlidis, Nicolaos Constantinides Th., Nikolaos Kokkas, George Pavlidis, and Stella Markantonatou. 2022. Morphologically annotated corpora of Pomak. In *Proceedings of the Fifth Workshop on the Use of Computational Methods in the Study of Endangered Languages*, pages 179–186.

Dan Kondratyuk and Milan Straka. 2019. 75 languages, 1 model: Parsing Universal Dependencies universally. In *Proceedings of the 2019 Conference on Empirical Methods in Natural Language Processing and the 9th International Joint Conference on Natural Language Processing (EMNLP-IJCNLP)*, pages 2779–2795, Hong Kong, China. Association for Computational Linguistics.

Panagiotis G. Krimpas. 2020. Language and origin of Pomaks in the light of the Balkan Sprachbund. In A. Bartsiokas & N. Macha-Bizoumi M. Varvounis, editor, *The Pomaks of Thrace: Multidisciplinary and interdisciplinary approaches*, pages 167–204. Thessaloniki: K&M Stamoulis.

Minh Van Nguyen, Viet Dac Lai, Amir Pouran Ben Veyseh, and Thien Huu Nguyen. 2021. Trankit: A light-weight transformer-based toolkit for multilingual natural language processing. In *Proceedings of the 16th Conference of the European Chapter of the Association for Computational Linguistics: System Demonstrations*, pages 80–90, Online. Association for Computational Linguistics.

Peng Qi, Yuhao Zhang, Yuhui Zhang, Jason Bolton, and Christopher D. Manning. 2020. Stanza: A python natural language processing toolkit for many human languages. In *Proceedings of the 58th Annual Meeting of the Association for Computational Linguistics: System Demonstrations*, pages 101–108, Online. Association for Computational Linguistics.

Burr Settles. 2009. Active learning literature survey. Computer Sciences Technical Report 1648, University of Wisconsin–Madison.

Tianze Shi, Adrian Benton, Igor Malioutov, and Ozan Irsoy. 2021. Diversity-aware batch active learning for dependency parsing. *arXiv preprint arXiv:2104.13936.*

Milan Straka, Jan Hajič, and Jana Straková. 2016. UDPipe: Trainable pipeline for processing CoNLL-U files performing tokenization, morphological analysis, POS tagging and parsing. In *Proceedings of the Tenth International Conference on Language Resources and Evaluation (LREC'16)*, pages 4290–4297, Portorož, Slovenia. European Language Resources Association (ELRA).

Daniel Zeman, Jan Hajič, Martin Popel, Martin Potthast, Milan Straka, Filip Ginter, Joakim Nivre, and Slav Petrov. 2018. CoNLL 2018 shared task: Multilingual parsing from raw text to Universal Dependencies. In *Proceedings of the CoNLL 2018 Shared Task: Multilingual Parsing from Raw Text to Universal Dependencies*, pages 1–21, Brussels, Belgium. Association for Computational Linguistics.

Analysis of Corpus-based Word-Order Typological Methods

Diego Alves
Faculty of Humanities and
Social Sciences - University of Zagreb
dfvalio@ffzg.hr

Božo Bekavac
Faculty of Humanities and
Social Sciences - University of Zagreb
bbekavac@ffzg.hr

Daniel Zeman
Faculty of Mathematics and Physics
Charles University
zeman@ufal.mff.cuni.cz

Marko Tadić
Faculty of Humanities and
Social Sciences - University of Zagreb
marko.tadic@ffzg.hr

Abstract

This article presents a comparative analysis of four different syntactic typological approaches applied to 20 different languages. We compared three specific quantitative methods, using parallel CoNLL-U corpora, to the classification obtained via syntactic features provided by a typological database (lang2vec). First, we analyzed the Marsagram linear approach which consists of extracting the frequency word-order patterns regarding the position of components inside syntactic nodes. The second approach considers the relative position of heads and dependents, and the third is based simply on the relative position of verbs and objects. From the results, it was possible to observe that each method provides different language clusters which can be compared to the classic genealogical classification (the lang2vec and the head and dependent methods being the closest). As different word-order phenomena are considered in these specific typological strategies, each one provides a different angle of analysis to be applied according to the precise needs of the researchers.

1 Introduction

Typology is usually described as language classification regarding structural types. Its scope can be defined as the quest for answers about how languages differ from each other, and about the explanation for the attested differences and similarities.

In terms of syntactic typology, one possible linguistic aspect that is analyzed concerns word-order patterns. These phenomena are commonly used to define sets of typological universals in terms of implications, correlations, and universals.

Most studies in this field rely on the identification of the most frequent word-order phenomena in different languages. Although based on attested syntactic constructions, what is extracted from the available linguistic data concerns only the most common syntactic structures. Thus, possible word-order patterns which are not the standard ones are usually ignored in these analyses. It is the case of the syntactic information provided by standard typological databases such as WALS (Dryer and Haspelmath, 2013). Although limited, these databases provide valuable information for theoretical typological analyses and can be used to improve the effectiveness of Natural Language Processing (NLP) tools, as shown by (Ponti et al., 2019).

On the other hand, corpus-based typological studies can provide a more precise description in terms of possible syntactic phenomena, thus, allowing languages to be compared in a more detailed way, as presented by (Levshina, 2022). Quantitative methods can be used in the analysis of numerous linguistic phenomena, and, even though they can present some bias regarding the corpora selection and annotation, they provide new insights that can challenge and/or complement classic theoretical approaches.

The aim of this article is to propose three different corpus-based quantitative methods concerning word-order typology and compare the obtained language classifications to the one provided by the comparison of the syntactic features provided from a typological database. The objective is to show that different approaches provide valuable but diverse contributions in terms of word-order structures attested in annotated corpora.

The paper is composed as follows: Section 2 presents an overview of the related work to this topic. Section 3 describes the campaign design: the language and data-set selection and the syntactic typological approaches; Section 4 present the obtained results which are discussed in Section 5. In Section 6 we provide conclusions and possible future directions for the research.

2 Related Work

According to (Ponti et al., 2019), the WALS database is one of the most used typological resources in NLP studies as it contains phonolog-

Proceedings of the Sixth Workshop on Universal Dependencies (UDW, GURT/SyntaxFest 2023), pages 36 - 46
March 9-12, 2023 ©2023 Association for Computational Linguistics

ical, morphosyntactic, and lexical information for a large number of languages. Besides that, the URIEL Typological Compendium is a meta-repository composed of several databases (WALS included) and is the base of the lang2vec tool (Littell et al., 2017). This specific resource provides typological information about languages in the format of feature and value pairs. Thus languages can be represented by vectors which are composed of the selected linguistic information required by the user (e.g.: genealogical, phonological, syntactic, etc). One problem usually observed in these databases is the fact that they suffer from discrepancies that are caused by their variety of sources. Therefore, comparisons can only be made if the selected languages have values for the ensemble of chosen features. Furthermore, there are many gaps as not all languages have the same amount of descriptive literature. Moreover, as previously mentioned, most databases fail to illustrate the variations that can occur within a single language (i.e.: only the most frequent phenomena are reported, and not all possible ones). On the other hand, quantitative methods, such as the ones proposed in this article, provide precise information regarding the frequency of all attested word-order phenomena inside the analyzed corpora.

An extended survey of corpora-based typological studies was provided by (Levshina, 2022). While certain authors quantitively analyzed specific word-order patterns (e.g.: subject, verb, and object position (Östling, 2015), and verb and locative phrases (Wälchli, 2009)), other authors have focused on quantitative analyses regarding language complexity (e.g.: (Hawkins, 2003) and (Sinnemäki, 2014)).

With the aim of examining diachronic syntactic changes that characterize the evolution from Latin to Romance languages, (Liu and Xu, 2012) proposed a quantitative approach to analyze the distributions of dependency directions. In total, 15 modern languages (8 Romance languages and 7 from other families) and 2 ancient ones (Latin and Ancient Greek) were scrutinized by the extraction of syntactic information from annotated corpora. The attested dependency syntactic networks for each language were analyzed with the calculation of certain syntactic parameters extracted from each corpus (i.e.: the mean sentential length, the percentage of the head-final dependencies, the head-initial dependencies, the dependencies between adjacent words, and of dependencies between non-adjacent words, the mean distance of all head-final dependencies, and the mean distance of all head-initial dependencies). It has been shown that the dependency syntactic networks arising from the selected data-sets reflect the degree of inflectional variation of each language. The adopted clustering approach also allowed Romance languages to be differentiated from Latin diachronically and between each other synchronically. However, the authors used data from the shared tasks of CoNLL 2006 (Buchholz and Marsi, 2006) and CoNLL 2007 (Nivre et al., 2007), however the dependency annotation schemes differed substantially from each other, so any studies based on those treebanks were problematic.

Another method concerning the extraction and comparison of syntactic information from treebanks was proposed by (Blache et al., 2016a). They developed the Marsagram tool, a resource that allows typological syntactic information (together with its statistics) to be obtained by inferring context-free grammars from syntactic structures inside annotated corpora. In terms of word-order, this tool allows the extraction of linear patterns (i.e.: if a specific part-of-speech precedes another one inside the same node of the syntactic tree governed by a determined head). The authors conducted a cluster analysis comparing 10 different languages and showed the potential in terms of typological analysis of this resource. However, the results were only compared to the genealogical classification of the selected languages and did not provide any comparison to other quantitative methods. Thus, one of the corpus-based typological approaches to be examined and compared in this article concerns the linear patterns provided by Marsagram tool.

The concept of Typometrics was introduced by (Gerdes et al., 2021). The authors extracted rich details for testing typological implicational universals and explored new kinds of universals, named quantitative universals. In their study, different word-order phenomena were analyzed quantitatively (i.e.: the distribution of their occurrences in annotated corpora) to identify universals (i.e.: present in all or most languages). Our approach differs from theirs as our aim is not to identify these implications or correlations but to compare languages (i.e.: language vectors) using all syntactic structures identified in the corpora to obtain a more general syntactic overview of the elements in our language set.

What is possible to observe in many studies regarding corpus-based typology is that usually a method is presented without a specific comparison to the existing approaches or to the classic one concerning the typological databases. Moreover, usually, the selected corpora are not completely homogeneous in terms of size or genre. Thus, in this study, the idea is to compare 20 different languages by using parallel corpora. (Levshina, 2022) showed the benefit of using this type of data, as the bias regarding size and content is avoided. Especially in this case, where syntactic patterns are the center of the analysis, the usage of parallel sentences allows the focus to be on the syntactic strategies that are used by each language to express the same meaning. Our objective is not to determine which is the best corpus-based approach, but to show how data can be explored from different angles, allowing typological nuances to be analyzed in detail.

3 Campaign Design

In this section, a brief overview of the selected datasets is provided, followed by a complete description of the syntactic typological approaches which were selected to conduct the corpus-based word-order analyses.

3.1 Parallel Corpora

The Parallel Universal Dependencies (PUD) compilation is an ensemble of tree-banks (parallel annotated corpora following Universal Dependencies guidelines (De Marneffe et al., 2021)) that was developed for the CoNLL 2017 shared task on Multilingual Parsing from Raw Text to Universal Dependencies (Zeman et al., 2018). It provides 1,000 parallel sentences from news sources and Wikipedia annotated in the CoNLL-U format for twenty languages[1]: Arabic, Chinese, Czech, English, Finnish, French, German, Hindi, Icelandic, Indonesian, Italian, Japanese, Korean, Polish, Portuguese, Russian, Spanish, Swedish, Thai, and Turkish. As previously explained, we decided to conduct the experiments with parallel annotated corpora to avoid biases regarding semantic content and size. However, as the PUD corpora are composed of translations from English (750 sentences), German (100), French (50), Spanish (50), and Italian (50), they may contain some "translationese" biases as described by (Volansky et al., 2015). Dependency parsing annotations were done automatically and, then, verified manually.

The list of PUD languages together with their ISO 639-3 codes and their genealogical and geographical information[2] is provided in Table 1.

The number of languages in this study is limited to 20 as we decided to focus on parallel data analysis. However, PUD collection provides, at least, some variety in terms of genealogy (i.e.: the great majority belongs to the Indo-European family, but 8 other different linguistic families are also present in this data-set). In terms of geographical areas, most languages are from the Eurasia region, the exceptions are Arabic (Africa), Chinese, Indonesian, and Thai (these 3 being from Southeast and Oceania region). The geographical areas presented in this article correspond to the ones described by (Dryer, 1992) and contain some discrepancies when compared to the ones proposed by WALS (Dryer and Haspelmath, 2013) (e.g.: while (Dryer, 1992) considers Arabic as an African language, in WALS, it is associated to Eurasia geographical area).

The PUD Collection used in this article corresponds to the one available in the Universal Dependencies data-set v.2.7 (November 2020).

3.2 Typological Approaches

The main idea is to generate, for each method, language vectors whose features correspond to specific word-order features and the values, to the frequency of the syntactic phenomenon in each corpus. With these vectors, languages are compared using Euclidean distance measures, generating dissimilarity matrices that can be, later, visually analyzed using a clustering algorithm.

The obtained classifications using the quantitative strategies are compared to the one provided by the clustering analysis conducted with typological information (syntactic features) provided by lang2vec tool (i.e.: the lang2vec classification is considered as our baseline).

Three typological approaches were chosen:

- Marsagram linear patterns
- Head and Dependent relative position
- Verb and Object relative position

[1] Originally it contained fewer languages, for example, Polish and Icelandic were added after the shared task.

[2] Although the existence of the Altaic family has been challenged by some experts as detailed by (Norman, 2009), WALS database consider it in its genealogical classification.

Language	ISO 639-3	Family	Genus	Geographical Area
Arabic	arb	Afro-Asiatic	Semitic	Africa
Chinese	cmn	Sino-Tibetan	Chinese	Southeast Asia and Oceania
Czech	ces	Indo-European	Slavic	Eurasia
English	eng	Indo-European	Germanic	Eurasia
Finnish	fin	Uralic	Finnic	Eurasia
French	fra	Indo-European	Romance	Eurasia
German	deu	Indo-European	Germanic	Eurasia
Hindi	hin	Indo-European	Indic	Eurasia
Icelandic	isl	Indo-European	Germanic	Eurasia
Indonesian	ind	Austronesian	Malayo-Sumbawan	Southeast Asia and Oceania
Italian	ita	Indo-European	Romance	Eurasia
Japanese	jpn	Japanese	Japanese	Eurasia
Korean	kor	Korean	Korean	Eurasia
Polish	pol	Indo-European	Slavic	Eurasia
Portuguese	por	Indo-European	Romance	Eurasia
Russian	rus	Indo-European	Slavic	Eurasia
Spanish	spa	Indo-European	Romance	Eurasia
Swedish	swe	Indo-European	Germanic	Eurasia
Thai	tha	Tai-Kadai	Kam-Tai	Southeast Asia and Oceania
Turkish	tur	Altaic	Turkic	Eurasia

Table 1: List of languages inside PUD collection, their respective ISO 639-3 three-character code, their genealogical information according to WALS, and the Geographical Area provided by (Dryer, 1992)

More details regarding the lang2vec analysis and each one of the new approaches are provided in the following sub-sections.

Thus, for each method, we first generate the 20 language vectors relative to the ensemble of PUD languages. Then, using the dist() R function, we obtain the dissimilarity matrices which are used for the clustering analysis.

In terms of hierarchical clustering methods, the Ward linkage method (Ward Jr, 1963) is applied to the obtained dissimilarity matrices. This strategy, instead of minimizing possible distances between pairs of clusters, minimizes the sum of squared differences within all clusters, thus, being a variance-minimizing approach. This agglomeration strategy has been chosen as its efficiency has been proven in many studies in the field of corpus-based linguistics and related disciplines (Eder, 2017). With the programming language R, it is possible to generate language clusters using the chosen linkage method with the function hclust() and the specific argument (method="ward.D2").

In the Results section, the different clustering classifications are presented, analyzed, and compared.

3.2.1 Lang2vec

As mentioned before, the lang2vec tool (Littell et al., 2017) is a valuable resource that provides typological information in the format of language vectors. In our case, lang2vec syntactic vectors are used. They describe languages morphosyntactically with information coming from the WALS database (Dryer and Haspelmath, 2013), the Syntactic Structures of World Languages (SSWL)[3], and Ethnologue [4].

In terms of syntactic features, the average vector (i.e.: compiling all possible features from the different databases) is composed of 103 features. The number of valid features (i.e.: with a specific value associated with it) varies from language to language. Each feature can receive the following values:

- 0.00 – the absence of the phenomenon
- 0.33 – the phenomenon can be observed but is not common
- 0.50 – the phenomenon is commonly observed together with other possible word-orders

[3]http://sswl.railsplayground.net/
[4]https://www.ethnologue.com/

- 0.67 – the phenomenon is relatively common.

- 1.00 – the phenomenon is normally encountered in the language.

There is a great discrepancy in terms of the availability of syntactic information regarding lang2vec syntactic features among PUD languages. It varies from 66 valid features for Arabic to 103 for English. Moreover, when checking the number of common valid features of all PUD languages, the final amount is 41 (i.e.: lang2vec PUD language vectors have 41 dimensions).

In terms of word-order phenomena described by the 41 common features composing the lang2vec PUD vectors, they correspond to:

- Subject, verb, and object (e.g.: SVO, SOV, SUBJECT_BEFORE_VERB)

- Adposition and noun (e.g.: ADPOSITION_BEFORE_NOUN)

- Possessor and noun (e.g.: POSSESSOR_AFTER_NOUN)

- Adjective and noun (e.g.: ADJECTIVE_AFTER_NOUN)

- Demonstrative and noun (e.g.: DEMONSTRATIVE_WORD_BEFORE_NOUN)

- Numeral and noun (e.g.: NUMERAL_AFTER_NOUN)

- Negative word and verb (e.g.: NEGATIVE_WORD_BEFORE_VERB)

- Degree word and adjective (e.g.: DEGREE_WORD_BEFORE_ADJECTIVE)

- Subordinator word and clause (e.g.: SUBORDINATOR_WORD_AFTER_CLAUSE)

- Polar question particle position: initial or final (e.g.: POLARQ_MARK_INITIAL)

- Existence of demonstrative prefix or suffix (e.g.: DEMONSTRATIVE_PREFIX)

- Existence of negative prefix or suffix (e.g.: NEGATIVE_PREFIX)

- Existence of TEND prefix or suffix (e.g.: TEND_SUFFIX)

- Existence of case mark, enclitic, proclitic, prefix, and suffix (e.g.: CASE_ENCLITIC)

We decided to use all the syntactic features available in lang2vec which are common to all PUD languages even if some of them are not directly related to word-order phenomena because when lang2vec vectors are used for experiments regarding the improvement of Natural Language Processing results, the whole set of lang2vec features is used.

3.2.2 Marsagram Linear Patterns

Marsagram is a tool for exploring treebanks, it extracts context-free grammars (CFG) from annotated data-sets that allow statistical comparison between languages as proposed by (Blache et al., 2016b). We have used the latest release of this software[5] available in the ORTOLANG platform of linguistic tools and resources.

This software identifies four types of properties: precede, require, exclude, and unicity. However, since the focus of this study is on word-order patterns, only "precede" property (linear) is considered. The extracted syntactic patterns contain information concerning part-of-speech and dependency parsing labels as well as the associated property type.

For example, *NOUN_precede_DET-det_NOUN-nmod* which means that a *DET* which has the dependency relation *det* precedes a *NOUN* with *nmod* as dependency label in the context of a node having *NOUN* as the head. An example of a sentence with this pattern is presented in the Appendix section (Figure 5). For each identified word-order phenomenon, Marsagram also indicates its frequency inside the corpus.

As expected, some patterns are common to all languages and some of them appear only in one or a few corpora. Therefore, the typological classification provided here concerns all possible identified rules (with an associated frequency value equal to zero for languages in which the pattern does not appear). In total, 21,242 linear patterns are extracted from the PUD collection (i.e.: the union of all patterns identified in PUD languages). The average amount of patterns with a frequency different from 0 is 15,790. However, even though only parallel corpora are considered, the number of extracted properties occurring in the corpora varies considerably among different languages: less than 10,000 for Japanese and Korean and more than 20,000 for English, Hindi, and Icelandic. The other PUD languages have a number of properties closer to the

[5]https://www.ortolang.fr/market/tools/ortolang-000917

average.

All the linear patterns that were identified with the Marsagram tool were considered when building the language vectors, even if they do not represent real dependency structures (e.g.: coordination phenomena). The main focus of the research is to obtain different quantitative typological classifications which can be used for dependency parsing improvement, thus, it is relevant to keep all the identified patterns.

3.2.3 Head and Dependent Relative Position

To analyze the dependency parsing results obtained from different languages using parallel corpora, we propose a quantitative typological approach concerning syntax, more specifically the head directionality parameter, whether the head precedes the dependent (right-branching) or is after it (left-branching) in the sentence (Fábregas et al., 2015). The extraction of parameters reflects the directionality observed at the surface level (position of head and dependent observed at the sentence level).

Thus, using a python script, the attested head and dependent relative position patterns are extracted together with their frequency of occurrence in each corpus. All observed features extracted from the PUD corpora (2,890 in total) have been included in the language vectors. In the cases where a feature is not observed in a determined corpus, the value 0 is attributed to it.

Two examples of head and dependent relative position patterns are presented below:

- ADV_advmod_precedes_ADJ - head-final or left-branching - It means that the dependent, which is an adverb (ADV) precedes the head which is an adjective (ADJ) and has the syntactic function of an adverbial modifier (advmod). The dependent can be in any position of the sentence previous to the head, not necessarily right before. An example of a sentence with this pattern is presented in the Appendix section (Figure 6).

- NOUN_obl_follows_VERB - head-initial or right-branching - In this case, the dependent (NOUN), comes after the head, which is a verb, and has the function of oblique nominal (obl). The dependent can be in any position after the head, not necessarily being right next to it. An example of a sentence representing this pattern is presented in the Appendix (Figure 7).

The analysis of these patterns corresponds to a quantitative approach of the Head and Dependent theory (Hawkins, 1983) which considers that there is a tendency of organizing head and dependents in homogeneous word ordering. (Hawkins, 1983) proposed a set of language types according to specific word-order phenomena concerning a limited list of heads and dependents. In this study, we consider all possible head and dependent pairs to compare the languages and classify them.

3.2.4 Verb and Object relative position

The verb (V) and direct object (O) relative position is part of the analysis regarding the heads and dependents ordering. We decided to analyze specifically the position of these two elements as they are key in typological studies such as the one proposed by (Dryer, 1992) where the correlations are defined according to whether in a language the verb comes before or after the object (i.e.: dependency relation "obj").

Thus, to compose the language vectors we extracted the head and dependent patterns which concern verbs and objects only (not only nominal but all other possible ones). The idea is to go beyond the classical approaches which usually consider only nominal objects (e.g.: (Dryer, 1992)) to see how languages are classified if all possible direct objects are analyzed. In total, 13 OV and 12 VO features were attested in the PUD collection, allowing us to generate a 25-dimension language vector for each language.

4 Results

As explained previously, each one of the presented typological methods generates a cluster dendrogram which is displayed in this section (Figures 1 to 4).

Starting with the lang2vec dendrogram (1), it is possible to notice that the central cluster is divided into two sub-groups (one composed of Chinese, English, and Swedish, and the other of Finnish, German, Icelandic, and the Slavic PUD languages). Arabic is classified in the same sub-group as Indonesian and Romance languages.

It is also noticeable that Hindi, Korean, Japanese, and Turkish form an isolated cluster. Moreover, Germanic languages are split into two sub-clusters, one formed by English and Swedish, together with Chinese, and the other composed of German and Icelandic (grouped with Slavic languages). Regarding this specific genus, although Polish and

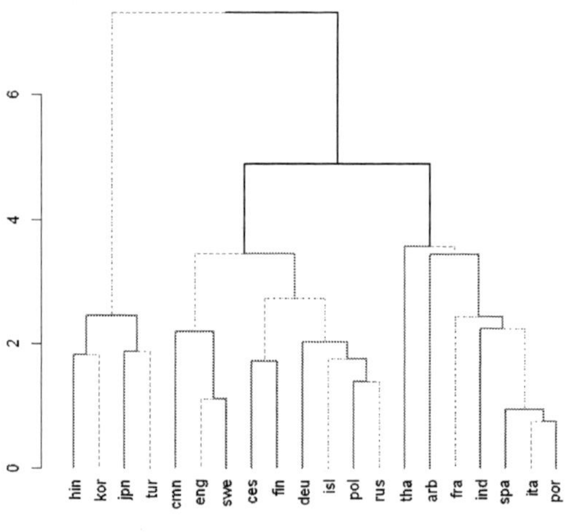

Figure 1: Lang2vec Clustering Dendrogram

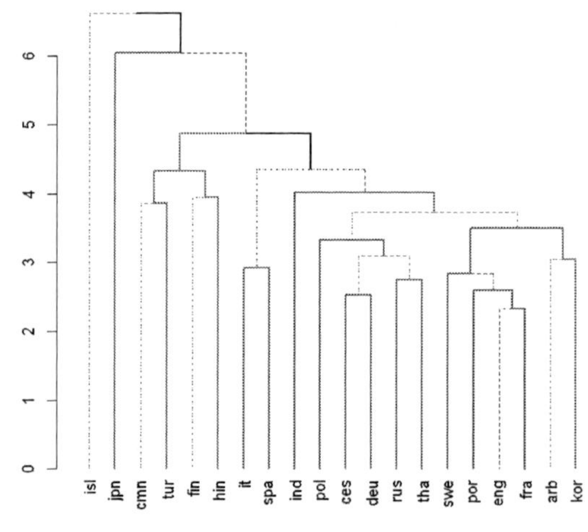

Figure 2: Marsagram Linear Properties Clustering Dendrogram

Russian are closer in both dendrograms, Czech is positioned closer to Finnish. Furthermore, as previously mentioned, when considering only lang2vec syntactic features, Thai and Arabic are classified as closer to Romance languages when compared to the others in the PUD collection.

If we consider the 3 main clusters provided by this dendrogram, it is possible to analyze which syntactic lang2vec features are shared by its languages. The isolated cluster formed by Hindi, Japanese, Korean and Turkish is composed of SOV languages with postpositions and with adjectives before nouns. The middle cluster (i.e.: Slavic and Germanic languages, plus Chinese and Finnish) has SVO languages with adjectives before nouns. And, finally, the cluster on the right side of the dendrograms is composed of VO (but not necessarily SVO) languages with prepositions and adjectives after the noun. Moreover, this cluster differs from the one located on the extreme left side of the dendrograms by ordering the negative word before the verb.

The analysis of the dendrogram concerning Marsagram linear patterns (2) shows Icelandic as an isolated language inside PUD collection. Japanese is also quite isolated from the other languages, however with lower distance values than Icelandic. Chinese, Turkish, Finnish, and Hindi form one small central cluster, as well as Italian and Spanish, and the other languages are grouped altogether. For this specific representation, languages from the same family or genus are not always clustered together (e.g.: Portuguese and Spanish, which formed a sub-cluster in lang2vec dendrograms in this case).

The large purple cluster is composed of Romance, Slavic, and Germanic languages (except Icelandic), but it also includes Indonesian, Arabic, Thai and Korean. Subject, Verb, and Object positions are not relevant criteria in this type of language classification. Marsagram extracts word-order patterns between elements that are part of the same syntactic node, thus, these components are not necessarily syntactically related.

When considering the classification provided by the dendrogram obtained with the head and dependent patterns (3), we observe that the Romance languages form one single isolated cluster positioned on the left side of the figure. On the other hand, the Germanic sub-group is closer to the Slavic one (with Icelandic being positioned inside the Slavic cluster and not with the other Germanic PUD languages). It is also noticeable that Thai, Arabic, and Indonesian form a specific sub-group closer to the Germanic and Slavic languages.

Japanese is clustered with Hindi and closer to other OV languages (i.e.: Turkish and Korean). The large cluster containing all OV languages from PUD also includes Finnish and Chinese which are not OV. When compared to the genealogical clas-

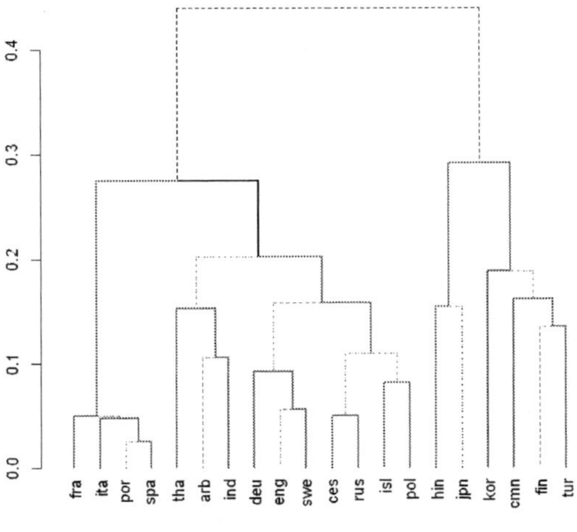

Figure 3: Head and Dependent relative position Clustering Dendrogram

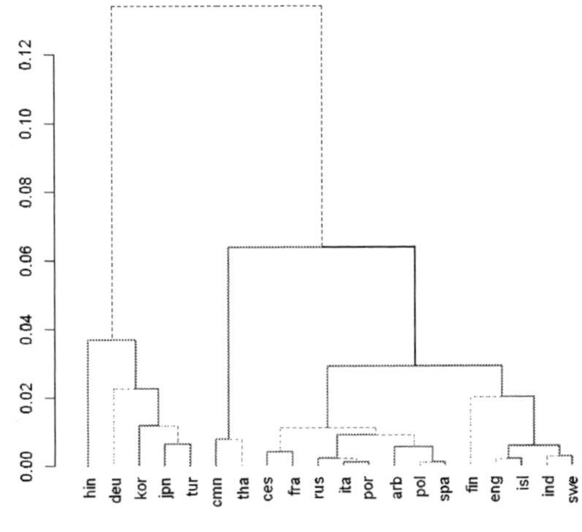

Figure 4: Verb and Object relative position Clustering Dendrogram

sification of PUD languages, it is possible to see that the proximity between Spanish and Portuguese and their relation to French and Italian is also present when the head and dependent orderings are examined. Icelandic is genealogically closer to Swedish, however, in terms of head directionality it is closer to Slavic languages, this classification is closer to the one proposed by (Hawkins, 1983): Icelandic, Czech, and Russian are all considered as type 10. Nevertheless, still according to (Hawkins, 1983), Indonesian and Thai are from the same language type as Romance languages (type 9), but in these dendrograms, although these two languages are grouped together, they are not classed among Romance ones. Moreover, although not genealogically related, the syntactic proximity between Finnish and Turkish is similarly attested with the head directionality analysis.

As expected, when VO and OV patterns are used to generate a dendrogram (4), there is a clear split of PUD languages into two clusters: one contains all OV languages and German (with no dominant order, according to WALS database), and the other, all the VO languages. When analyzing VO languages in detail, it is noticeable that French and Czech are closer in the Verb and Object relative position dendrogram. Finnish is placed together with Germanic languages (except for German) and Indonesian. Slavic languages (except for Czech) are clustered with Romance languages (except for French) in a sub-group that also contains Arabic. The Thai language forms a small sub-cluster with Chinese.

As not only nominal objects are considered for the construction of this dendrogram, it also provides also insights into how other types of objects are ordered (e.g.: pronominal). Thus, this classification cannot be compared to the one provided by (Hawkins, 1983) where only nominal objects were analyzed.

The overall analysis of all obtained dendrograms shows that both lang2vec and head and dependent position figures have more similarities to the classical genealogical classification of languages. Marsagram dendrogram clearly presents a specific typological classification that considers word-order phenomena not contemplated by the other analysis. The verb and object classification provides a particular typological overview that can be interesting for studying focusing on how these two elements are positioned.

In comparison with the language types proposed by (Hawkins, 1983), the typological classifications presented in this article present the advantage of allowing languages to be compared in terms of a larger number of word-order structures, thus, being more precise for NLP applications where the objective is to find the closest languages. For example, as previously mentioned, Indonesian and Thai are classified as type 9 by (Hawkins, 1983), the same group as the PUD Romance languages. However, using the described quantitative methods it is possible to determine how close these two languages are to the Romance ones in a more detailed way.

5 Conclusion and Perspectives

In this paper, we presented three new typological approaches regarding word-order phenomena applied to 20 different languages using parallel corpora. The new methods were compared to the standard one which considers syntactic features provided by a typological database (lang2vec).

Each approach provided a syntactic typological classification of languages in the format of a dendrogram which was obtained via dissimilarity matrices composed of Euclidean distances between language vectors.

We showed that each different approach has its own particularities. The aim of this study was not to state which is the best typological method but to show in which way they provide different angles for typological analysis. However, it is possible to notice that the lang2vec and the Head and Dependent relative position dendrograms are more coherent with the genealogical classification of languages. The Marsagram approach provides interesting aspects regarding specific word-order phenomena of elements that are not syntactically related, while the Verb and Object relative position approach provides a specific analysis of all attested phenomena regarding these elements.

The usability of each method depends on which particular syntactic features are of interest and the purpose of further linguistic processing. Preliminary experiments showed that the language distances obtained using the described quantitative typological methods present moderate or strong correlations with the improvement of dependency parsing results when different languages are combined to train deep-learning models. Thus, in the future, we aim to analyze precisely how each method provides valuable information concerning the improvement of the dependency parsing results to determine the best corpus-based typological strategy for this aim.

Acknowledgements

The work presented in this paper has received funding from the European Union's Horizon 2020 research and innovation program under the Marie Skłodowska-Curie grant agreement no. 812997 and under the name CLEOPATRA (Cross-lingual Event-centric Open Analytics Research Academy).

References

Philippe Blache, Stéphane Rauzy, and Grégoire Montcheuil. 2016a. Marsagram: an excursion in the forests of parsing trees. In *Language Resources and Evaluation Conference*, 10, page 7.

Philippe Blache, Stéphane Rauzy, and Grégoire Montcheuil. 2016b. MarsaGram: an excursion in the forests of parsing trees. In *Proceedings of the Tenth International Conference on Language Resources and Evaluation (LREC'16)*, pages 2336–2342, Portorož, Slovenia. European Language Resources Association (ELRA).

Sabine Buchholz and Erwin Marsi. 2006. Conll-x shared task on multilingual dependency parsing. In *Proceedings of the tenth conference on computational natural language learning (CoNLL-X)*, pages 149–164.

Marie-Catherine De Marneffe, Christopher D Manning, Joakim Nivre, and Daniel Zeman. 2021. Universal dependencies. *Computational linguistics*, 47(2):255–308.

Matthew S Dryer. 1992. The greenbergian word order correlations. *Language*, 68(1):81–138.

Matthew S. Dryer and Martin Haspelmath, editors. 2013. *WALS Online*. Max Planck Institute for Evolutionary Anthropology, Leipzig.

Maciej Eder. 2017. Visualization in stylometry: cluster analysis using networks. *Digital Scholarship in the Humanities*, 32(1):50–64.

Antonio Fábregas, Jaume Mateu, and Michael T. Putnam. 2015. *Contemporary Linguistic Parameters: Contemporary Studies in Linguistics*. Bloomsbury Academic, London.

Kim Gerdes, Bruno Guillaume, Sylvain Kahane, and Guy Perrier. 2021. Starting a new treebank? go SUD! In *Proceedings of the Sixth International Conference on Dependency Linguistics (Depling, SyntaxFest 2021)*, pages 35–46, Sofia, Bulgaria. Association for Computational Linguistics.

John A Hawkins. 1983. *Word order universals*, volume 3. Elsevier.

John A Hawkins. 2003. Efficiency and complexity in grammars: Three general principles. *The nature of explanation in linguistic theory*, 121:152.

Natalia Levshina. 2022. Corpus-based typology: applications, challenges and some solutions. *Linguistic Typology*, 26(1):129–160.

Patrick Littell, David R Mortensen, Ke Lin, Katherine Kairis, Carlisle Turner, and Lori Levin. 2017. Uriel and lang2vec: Representing languages as typological, geographical, and phylogenetic vectors. In *Proceedings of the 15th Conference of the European Chapter of the Association for Computational Linguistics: Volume 2, Short Papers*, pages 8–14.

Haitao Liu and Chunshan Xu. 2012. Quantitative typological analysis of romance languages. *Poznań Studies in Contemporary Linguistics*, 48(4):597–625.

Joakim Nivre, Johan Hall, Sandra Kübler, Ryan McDonald, Jens Nilsson, Sebastian Riedel, and Deniz Yuret. 2007. The conll 2007 shared task on dependency parsing. In *Proceedings of the 2007 Joint Conference on Empirical Methods in Natural Language Processing and Computational Natural Language Learning (EMNLP-CoNLL)*, pages 915–932.

Jerry Norman. 2009. A new look at altaic. *Journal of the American Oriental Society*, 129(1):83–89.

Robert Östling. 2015. Word order typology through multilingual word alignment. In *Proceedings of the 53rd Annual Meeting of the Association for Computational Linguistics and the 7th International Joint Conference on Natural Language Processing (Volume 2: Short Papers)*, pages 205–211.

Edoardo Maria Ponti, Helen O'Horan, Yevgeni Berzak, Ivan Vulić, Roi Reichart, Thierry Poibeau, Ekaterina Shutova, and Anna Korhonen. 2019. Modeling language variation and universals: A survey on typological linguistics for natural language processing. *Computational Linguistics*, 45(3):559–601.

Kaius Sinnemäki. 2014. Complexity trade-offs: A case study. In *Measuring grammatical complexity*, pages 179–201. Oxford University Press.

Vered Volansky, Noam Ordan, and Shuly Wintner. 2015. On the features of translationese. *Digital Scholarship in the Humanities*, 30(1):98–118.

Joe H Ward Jr. 1963. Hierarchical grouping to optimize an objective function. *Journal of the American statistical association*, 58(301):236–244.

Bernhard Wälchli. 2009. Data reduction typology and the bimodal distribution bias. 13(1):77–94.

Daniel Zeman, Jan Hajic, Martin Popel, Martin Potthast, Milan Straka, Filip Ginter, Joakim Nivre, and Slav Petrov. 2018. Conll 2018 shared task: Multilingual parsing from raw text to universal dependencies. In *Proceedings of the CoNLL 2018 Shared Task: Multilingual parsing from raw text to universal dependencies*, pages 1–21.

A Appendix

```
# text = Each map in the exhibition tells its own story, not all factual.
1   Each    each    DET DT  _   2   det 2:det   _
2   map map NOUN    NN  Number=Sing 6   nsubj   6:nsubj _
3   in  in  ADP IN  _   5   case    5:case  _
4   the the DET DT  Definite=Def|PronType=Art   5   det 5:det   _
5   exhibition  exhibition  NOUN    NN  Number=Sing 2   nmod    2:nmod:in   _
6   tells   tell    VERB    VBZ Mood=Ind|Number=Sing|Person=3|Tense=Pres|VerbForm=Fin   0   root    0:root  _
7   its its PRON    PRP$    Gender=Neut|Number=Sing|Person=3|Poss=Yes|PronType=Prs  9   nmod:poss   9:nmod:poss _
8   own own ADJ JJ  Degree=Pos  9   amod    9:amod  _
9   story   story   NOUN    NN  Number=Sing 6   obj 6:obj   SpaceAfter=No
10  ,   ,   PUNCT   ,   _   6   punct   6:punct _
11  not not ADV RB  Polarity=Neg    12  advmod  12:advmod   _
12  all all DET DT  _   13  nsubj   13:nsubj    _
13  factual factual ADJ JJ  Degree=Pos  6   parataxis   6:parataxis SpaceAfter=No
14  .   .   PUNCT   .   _   6   punct   6:punct _
```

Figure 5: Example of a sentence with the pattern NOUN_precede_DET-det_NOUN-nmod. The determiner (DET) on line 4 has the incoming relation det. It precedes the noun (NOUN) on line 5, which has the incoming relation nmod. Both appear in the subtree headed by a NOUN (the first tag in the pattern description); in this case, it is again the noun on line 5.

```
# text = These are not very popular due to the often remote and roadless locations.
1   These   these   PRON    DT  Number=Plur|PronType=Dem    5   nsubj   5:nsubj _
2   are be  AUX VBP Mood=Ind|Tense=Pres|VerbForm=Fin    5   cop 5:cop   _
3   not not PART    RB  Polarity=Neg    5   advmod  5:advmod    _
4   very    very    ADV RB  _   5   advmod  5:advmod    _
5   popular popular ADJ JJ  Degree=Pos  0   root    0:root  _
6   due due ADP IN  _   13  case    13:case _
7   to  to  ADP IN  _   6   fixed   6:fixed _
8   the the DET DT  Definite=Def|PronType=Art   13  det 13:det  _
9   often   often   ADV RB  _   10  advmod  10:advmod   _
10  remote  remote  ADJ JJ  Degree=Pos  13  amod    13:amod _
11  and and CCONJ   CC  _   12  cc  12:cc   _
12  roadless    roadless    ADJ JJ  Degree=Pos  10  conj    10:conj:and|13:amod _
13  locations   location    NOUN    NNS Number=Plur 5   obl 5:obl:due_to    SpaceAfter=No
14  .   .   PUNCT   .   _   5   punct   5:punct _
```

Figure 6: Example of a sentence with two occurrences of the pattern ADV_advmod_precedes_ADJ. The adverb (ADV) on line 9 has the incoming relation advmod. It precedes the adjective (ADJ) on line 10. And, the adverb (ADV) on line 4 has the incoming relation advmod. It precedes the adjective (ADJ) on line 5.

```
# text = The new spending is fueled by Clinton's large bank account.
1   The the DET DT  Definite=Def|PronType=Art   3   det 3:det   _
2   new new ADJ JJ  Degree=Pos  3   amod    3:amod  _
3   spending    spending    NOUN    NN  Number=Sing 5   nsubj:pass  5:nsubj:pass    _
4   is  be  AUX VBZ Mood=Ind|Number=Sing|Person=3|Tense=Pres|VerbForm=Fin   5   aux:pass    5:aux:pass  _
5   fueled  fuel    VERB    VBN Tense=Past|VerbForm=Part    0   root    0:root  _
6   by  by  ADP IN  _   11  case    11:case _
7   Clinton Clinton PROPN   NNP Number=Sing 11  nmod:poss   11:nmod:poss    SpaceAfter=No
8   's  's  PART    POS _   7   case    7:case  _
9   large   large   ADJ JJ  Degree=Pos  11  amod    11:amod _
10  bank    bank    NOUN    NN  Number=Sing 11  compound    11:compound _
11  account account NOUN    NN  Number=Sing 5   obl 5:obl:by    SpaceAfter=No
12  .   .   PUNCT   .   _   5   punct   5:punct _
```

Figure 7: Example of a sentence with the pattern NOUN_obl_follows_VERB. The noun (NOUN) on line 11 has the incoming relation obl. It comes after the verb (VERB) on line 5.

Rule-based semantic interpretation for Universal Dependencies

Jamie Y. Findlay and **Saeedeh Salimifar** and **Ahmet Yıldırım** and **Dag T. T. Haug**
Department of Linguistics and Nordic Studies
University of Oslo

Abstract

In this paper, we present a system for generating semantic representations from Universal Dependencies syntactic parses. The foundation of our pipeline is a rule-based interpretation system, designed to be as universal as possible, which produces the correct semantic structure; the content of this structure can then be filled in by additional (sometimes language-specific) post-processing. The rules which generate semantic resources rely as far as possible on the UD parse alone, so that they can apply to any language for which such a parse can be given (a much larger number than the number of languages for which detailed semantically annotated corpora are available). We discuss our general approach, and highlight areas where the UD annotation scheme makes semantic interpretation less straightforward. We compare our results with the Parallel Meaning Bank, and show that when it comes to modelling semantic structure, our approach shows potential, but also discuss some areas for expansion.

1 Introduction

Aside from the theoretical interest in discovering how syntactic information contributes to semantic interpretation, there are also a number of practical benefits to augmenting syntactic descriptions with semantic representations. A suitably rich semantic representation automatically makes possible a number of common downstream tasks such as named entity recognition, information retrieval, machine translation, and natural language inference. In this paper, we report on our system for using Universal Dependencies syntactic annotations (UD: Nivre et al., 2020) to produce semantic representations, in this case Discourse Representation Structures (DRSs: Kamp and Reyle, 1993; Kamp et al., 2011). Figure 1 shows the UD parse and a possible DRS representation for a simple sentence.

In particular, and unlike much of the state of the art, our pipeline makes heavy use of a rule-based

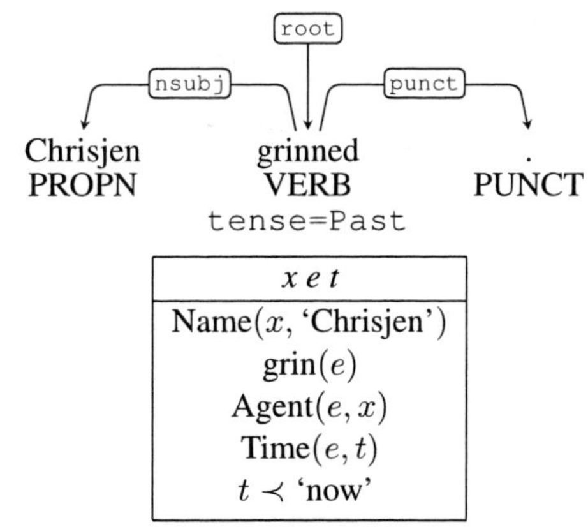

Figure 1: UD graph and DRS for *Chrisjen grinned*

component. This component inspects the UD graph and uses it to produce a number of *meaning constructors*, the basic building blocks of semantic composition in Glue Semantics (Glue: Dalrymple et al., 1993; Asudeh, 2022). Meaning constructors are pairs, the first element of which is a lambda expression in some meaning language, and the second element of which is a formula in linear logic (Girard, 1987) that expresses a type. The atoms of this linear logic statement are indexed with node labels, thereby anchoring (or 'gluing') the semantics to the syntax. This flexible approach to meaning composition allows each word to make any number of distinct meaning contributions, and frees composition from word order, making it a perfect fit for a dependency grammar like UD (see Haug and Findlay 2023).

Rules in our rule-based system consist of two parts: on the left-hand side, a description which nodes in the UD tree might satisfy (e.g. referring to the node's dependency relation, its lemma, or its features), and on the right-hand side, a meaning constructor to be introduced. This system has been implemented, using a Haskell script to inspect the UD tree node by node, comparing each one to the rules in our ruleset, and introducing the appropriate

Proceedings of the Sixth Workshop on Universal Dependencies (UDW, GURT/SyntaxFest 2023), pages 47 - 57
March 9-12, 2023 ©2023 Association for Computational Linguistics

meaning constructor each time a node matches a description (for more details on this process, albeit in a different syntactic setting, see Gotham and Haug 2018).[1]

Once a collection of meaning constructors has been obtained, they are passed to the Glue Semantics Workbench (Messmer and Zymla, 2018), which uses them to produce a linear logic proof (or proofs, in the case of scope ambiguities) whose conclusion is the meaning constructor corresponding to the semantic representation of the sentence. We subequently use the Python Natural Language Toolkit (NLTK: Garrette and Klein, 2009) to perform any post-processing steps, including producing human- and machine-readable DRS outputs.

Our system is part of an ongoing project on universal semantic parsing, and so another prominent feature of our system is its focus on broad coverage. This sets it apart from other works which combine symbolic and machine-learning approaches (e.g. Kalouli and Crouch 2018; Hu et al. 2020), since these are limited to specific languages, e.g. English, because specific tools exist, or to other languages for which there exist sufficient data to train a deep learning system. Because of the lack of semantically annotated training data for the majority of the world's languages, recent efforts in broad coverage semantic parsing (e.g. Liu et al. 2021) have been based on machine translation into English, followed by semantic parsing and projection of the result onto the source language. However, state of the art machine translation is only available for high-resource languages (Haddow et al., 2022) and is likely to introduce noise even in the best of cases, especially if the languages are typologically distant.

Instead of this translational approach, we try to leverage UD representations to achieve universality. As far as possible, our rule system produces meanings based exclusively on the UD parse, without invoking language- or lemma-specific rules. Section 2 discusses the kinds of rules used in more detail (and Section 3 identifies some issues that arise which are of potential relevance to UD as a framework). However, this language-neutral approach means that the output of the rule-based component is necessarily underspecified, since, for example, semantic roles (Agent, Patient, etc.) do not stand in a one-to-one correspondence with syntactic relations (`nsubj`, `obj`, etc.). For some languages, this is as far as we can go. But where languages have more resources available, and we can therefore access the language- and lemma-specific information needed, we can make use of various post-processing steps to further refine our semantic representations. One of these systems, used to convert syntactic labels for dependencies into appropriate semantic role labels, is described in Section 4.

In Section 5, we compare the output of our pipeline with an existing benchmark of DRS parsing, the Parallel Meaning Bank (PMB: Abzianidze et al., 2017). Our goals are slightly different from those of the PMB, so although this comparison offers indications about the adequacy of our rule system, it does not offer a perfect gold standard.

Moving forward, we have further plans for post-processing, and these are discussed in Section 6. We also indicate some limitations of the PMB dataset as a gold standard for DRS parsing.

2 Rules for semantic interpretation

By using a rule-based system, we can more easily import insights from theoretical linguistics into automatic semantic interpretation. These insights are generally of a structural nature: e.g. the fact that the logical structures produced by different quantifiers do not straightforwardly match their syntactic structure is the sort of thing that may be difficult for a machine-learning algorithm to infer.[2] At the same time, our universal goals mean that language-specific information, such as the semantic roles a predicate assigns to its arguments, must be abstracted away from, since we cannot retrieve this information from the UD parse alone. The target output of our rule-based system is therefore not a fully-specified DRS. Instead, we aim to produce a *structurally* accurate DRS, where the correct discourse referents are present and the hierarchical relations between them are correct; the *content* of the DRS, by which we mean the labels for the relations, or the word senses attributed to the discourse referents, will be filled in only later, by language-specific post-processing. Concretely, except for in the cases where no language-/lemma-specific information is required to determine the correct labels, our rule system outputs syntactic (rather than semantic) labels for the relations between discourse

[1] The code used for our system is available at `https://github.com/Universal-NLU/UNLU`, including a sample set of semantic interpretation rules.

[2] By contrast, tasks like word sense disambiguation, which rely on large numbers of sometimes subtle cues, are precisely those tasks for which machine-learning systems are well suited.

referents, and uses lemmas in place of word senses.

2.1 Target representations

As mentioned, our target semantic representations are DRSs. In order to facilitate comparison with an existing benchmark, we aim to follow the specific format of the Parallel Meaning Bank (PMB). This is a fairly standard meaning representation format based on a neo-Davidsonian event semantics whereby verbs denote predicates of events (or states) and participants in these events are connected via thematic role predicates like Agent and Patient that relate events and individuals (Davidson, 1967; Parsons, 1990). The PMB does make a few less standard choices, however. For example, it is less expressive than some semantic theories in that it has no representation of number (except for in the case of 1st and 2nd person pronouns); but it is also more expressive in that it annotates a basic level of presuppositional structure (based on Projective DRT: Venhuizen et al. 2013). Ultimately, we wish to improve on both of these areas, by incorporating an explicit representation of number, and by capturing more presupposition triggers, but for now we attempt to diverge as little as possible from the PMB representations, in order to facilitate comparison.

2.2 Types of rule

In this section, we illustrate a few categories of rule, divided by the kind of information they require from the UD parse.

2.2.1 Part of speech

For some situations, the part of speech tag alone is sufficient to determine the node's semantic contribution. This is the case for proper nouns, for example, since we know they will contribute a discourse referent that stands in the 'Name' relation to its lemma (its name). Our rule that captures this is shown as rule 1 in Figure 2 (we also employ a second rule, not shown, that provides a meaning constructor that turns this meaning into a generalised quantifier). If a node has the UD POS `PROPN`, then we introduce a meaning constructor of type `e(!) -o t(!)` that adds the appropriate condition to the DRS for the sentence. The semantic side of the meaning constructor is written in the DRS representation language of the NLTK. On the linear logic side, we use `!` and `^` to refer to the current node and its mother, respectively; these will be instantiated to numeric node indices in a specific parse. The string `-o` is used to represent the linear implication symbol $\multimap$; Glue Semantics uses linear logic to guide semantic composition, following the 'proofs-as-programs' paradigm enabled by the Curry-Howard isomorphism (Curry and Feys, 1958; Howard, 1980). So the linear logic expression in this rule tells us it has the type $\langle e, t\rangle$ and that it is anchored in the current node, the one with the POS `PROPN`.

2.2.2 UD tree

For other cases, the topography of the UD tree itself encodes the semantic information we wish to capture. For example, some syntactic dependencies are also semantic dependencies – arguments and adjuncts like `nsubj`, `obj`, `ccomp`, `obl`, etc. We therefore require a number of rules whereby the presence of such a dependency produces a meaning constructor that introduces a parallel semantic dependency. Rule 2 in Figure 2 shows an example for `nsubj` when it is a dependent of a verb. This rule has two conditions, joined by `;`, signifying conjunction: the UD dependency of the node must be `nsubj`, and its mother node must have the POS `VERB`. We employ a Champollion-style representation of verbal meanings such that they do not have the usual $\langle v, t\rangle$ type of properties of events, but rather the higher type $\langle\langle v, t\rangle, t\rangle$ (Champollion, 2015). To minimise clutter in our rules, we define a new type `x(n)` which is equivalent to `((v(n) -o t(n)) -o t(n))`. The meaning constructor in rule 2 therefore consumes a generalised quantifier and produces a modifier of verbs, which adds the verb to the scope of the quantifier, and connects the variable being quantified over to the verb's event variable via an `nsubj` relation.

Although in general we require language-specific valency lexica to know which semantic role labels to use in place of syntactic labels like `nsubj`, in some cases we can nonetheless incorporate word-level information to make our DRSs more informative. For example, for `obl` dependents which have a `case` daughter, we use the lemma of the target of `case` (i.e. the preposition name) to label the semantic relation, thus adding a degree of granularity which would otherwise be absent.

Not all syntactic dependencies also correspond to semantic dependencies, of course: more functional ones like `aux`, `cop`, `case`, etc. usually do not in themselves (i.e. merely by their presence) contribute semantic information that is not also

```
1. coarsePos = PROPN -> \X.(([], [Name(X, ':LEMMA:')])) : e(!) -o t(!)
2. relation = nsubj; ^ {coarsePos = VERB} ->
      \Q.\V.\F.(Q(\X.(V(\E.(([], [nsubj(E,X)]) + F(E)))))) :
      ((e(!) -o t(^)) -o t(^)) -o (x(^) -o x(^))
3. coarsePos = VERB; ~ aux; Tense = Pres ->
      \V.\F.(V(\E.(([T], [time(T), EQ(T, 'now'), Time(E, T)]) + F(E)))) : x(!) -o x(!)
```

Figure 2: Some semantic interpretation rules

represented elsewhere; rather, the targets of such dependencies contribute semantic information in other ways, such as via their features.

2.2.3 Features

The UD feature space is not as consistently or reliably employed in treebanks as the part of speech tags or dependency graph labels are, and so we use it only sparingly in our rule system. Nonetheless, there are certain cases where it supplies crucial information that saves us having to fall back on language-specific resources. For example, the tense of simplex verbs (those without auxiliaries) can be reliably read off the `Tense` feature, as rule 3 in Figure 2 illustrates for the present tense (the symbol ~ represents negation).

2.2.4 More complex constructions

Of course, such simple rules only get us so far. Other phenomena, such as coordination or negation, require a rich set of complex interacting rules. Coordination is made especially challenging by the fact that in UD there is no node which represents the coordinate structure as a whole, meaning that the line between properties of the whole structure and properties of the first conjunct is blurred. There are other complexities here too: for instance, our system currently assumes that coordination is only possible with identical UD relations (e.g. coordinated `obj`s), since the relationship between each conjunct and its semantic governor is mediated through the first conjunct, so whatever UD relation that word bears is assumed to be extended to the rest of the conjuncts. But of course this is empirically inadequate: as Przepiórkowski and Patejuk (2018) point out, in a sentence like *He asked her for a kiss and to go on a date with him* the first conjunct is an `obl` but the second would be annotated as an `xcomp` if it stood alone. Yet here it is merely a `conj` daughter of *kiss*, so it is not easy to reconstruct a different relationship with the verb than the one it bears indirectly via its mother. To some extent we can leverage the fact that UD relations are partly determined by the part of speech of the dependent: for example, a verbal `conj` dependent of a noun will be a `csubj` if the noun is `nsubj`. But if the noun is `obj`, the verbal conjunct can be `ccomp` or `xcomp` and we won't always have the morphological features to decide, especially not in a universal setting. Finally, if the noun is `obl`, as in the example from Przepiórkowski and Patejuk (2018), we run into the problem that UD makes an argument/adjunct distinction for clauses but not for noun phrases: if the sentence was *He did it for the money and to please his record company*, the infinitive would be `advcl`.

2.3 Challenges of universalism

To a large extent, our more targetted goal of obtaining the correct semantic *structure* while abstracting away from specific labels means that we do not rely on language-specific information, and therefore can develop a genuinely universal rule scheme which relies solely on properties of the UD parse. However, there are certain aspects of semantic structure where language-specific information may still be required. For example, the semantic structures arising from universal vs. existential quantifiers are different, and nothing in the UD parse encodes this distinction. We therefore maintain a small list of parameters whose values are language-specific lemmas which identify certain key words, such as the form of universal and existential quantifiers. We also currently encode the form of future auxiliaries (e.g. English *will*), infinitive markers (e.g. English *to*), and definite determiners (since we find that the use of features like `Definite=Def` or `PronType=Dem` in treebanks and parsers is inconsistent). When parsing a language which lacks this data, we default to more coarse-grained rules which rely more heavily on features, or simply collapse some distinctions.

Similarly, there can be high-level grammatical differences between languages, such as whether they employ ergative or accusative case-marking, or whether they make use of negative concord, which are also relevant to the task of building a semantic structure. To capture these, we parametrise some rules, so that we can specify for each language which version should apply. When handling a language for which we lack this information, we assume the most typologically common version of the rule.

There are also very low-level lexically determined properties of semantic structure, e.g. the well-known distinction between subject-control and object-control verbs like *promise* and *persuade*: the UD trees for sentences like *I promised Holden to come* and *I persuaded Holden to come* will be identical, but the semantic argument of the subordinate clause's verb is different in each case (*I* in the first, *Holden* in the second). Given our goals, such information will unfortunately be missed; the requirement that a UD parse produce a tree (as opposed to a more general kind of graph) means that the syntactic representation we start from is not as rich as it would be in other frameworks (since there is no re-entrancy, for example), and certain information is therefore simply not represented.

3 Implications for Universal Dependencies

3.1 Shallowness of representation

This relative shallowness of UD parses is a well-known shortcoming of the framework. Despite the putative advantages of working with more constrained trees rather than full-fledged graphs, we wish to add our voices to those who believe the costs of this limitation outweigh the benefits. If UD annotations included the controllers of `xcomps`, for instance, then the problem mentioned above would not arise, since the difference between *promise* and *persuade* would also be indicated syntactically. This is done in so-called Enhanced UD (cf. Schuster and Manning 2016), for instance, but the cross-linguistic coverage of Enhanced UD treebanks is currently *much* sparser than basic UD (contentful Enhanced UD annotations are only available for 31 out of the 213 UD treebanks, and of these only 22 contain annotations indicating the controllers of `xcomps`). Although there exist automatic 'enhancers' which can convert basic UD into Enhanced UD (e.g. Nyblom et al. 2013; Schuster and Manning 2016; Nivre et al. 2018; Bouma et al. 2020), they are either language-specific or quite rudimentary (see critique in Findlay and Haug 2021). While it would certainly be useful to produce more Enhanced UD treebanks, we do not think it is likely that this will happen on the same scale as the UD project generally, and it is especially unlikely for low-resource languages, so we continue to make use of the basic UD annotations in our universally-oriented project.

3.2 Pro-drop

The problem of missing controller annotations intersects with another problem, discussed by Patejuk and Przepiórkowski (2018) – that of unexpressed/ pro-dropped arguments. Since pro-dropped arguments are not present in the string, they are not included in a UD parse, and this makes semantic interpretation much more challenging. We must always allow for the possibility that there are additional discourse referents which are related to each predicate in an unspecified way; and without accessing language-specific valency information we have no way of knowing how many or what kind of dependents might have been omitted. This issue also means that control relations cannot be included even in Enhanced UD representations when the controller is itself an unexpressed argument. We therefore agree with Patejuk and Przepiórkowski (2018, 216ff.) and Przepiórkowski and Patejuk (2020, 205ff.) that the inclusion of empty nodes in the string to represent pro-dropped arguments would be a valuable addition to basic UD (and would also help with adding control annotations: see Findlay and Haug, 2021, 26f.)

3.3 Lexical focus of features

UD feature annotations are scrupulously limited to the word level. This is problematic when features of phrases emerge non-compositionally, e.g. in periphrasis. As the UD guidelines acknowledge, "If a tense is constructed periphrastically [...] and none of the participating words are specific to this tense, then the features will probably not directly reveal the tense".[3] In this view of things, features like `Tense` should be seen as morphological features: they describe nothing more than the form of individual words, which may happen to align with their syntactic/semantic properties, but if so then only incidentally. However, such a view is at odds with the guidelines' own definition of the `Tense` feature: "Tense is a feature that specifies the time when the action took/takes/will take place, in relation to a reference point". This is an emphatically semantic definition. But given the problem of periphrasis, the `Tense` feature cannot be

[3] `https://universaldependencies.org/u/feat/Tense.html`

given any definitive semantic interpretation; the presence of `Tense=Pres` in English, for example, does not guarantee any reference to present tense – one of the places it occurs is on *-ing* participles, even when used in the past, as in *They were singing*. And `Tense=Past` appears on passive participles in English (whatever the tense), since they share the same form as past participles (further evidence this is in fact a morphological feature). While it would be possible to write rules to translate each language's unique combinations of morphological forms into the correct tense interpretations, this clearly goes against the universal aims of our project, and of UD itself. We believe therefore that it would be advantageous for UD to adopt some notion of clause-level features for qualities such as tense which are not usefully localised at the word level, or to concede that such features are purely morphological, and do not encode the semantic information they are currently claimed to.

4 Post-processing

A full semantic representation contains many types of information that simply cannot be extracted from the UD tree, even with the aid of linguistically-informed rules. Typically, this is information that would be associated with lexical entries rather than with structural syntax.

The most prominent example of this kind is the mapping from syntactic functions to semantic roles: UD gives us labels like `nsubj`, `obj` etc., but how these map to roles like Agent, Patient, Stimulus, Experiencer, etc. is verb-specific. We resolve this mapping in a separate post-processing step, where for English we rely on VerbNet (Kipper et al., 2008), which provides details of the syntactic frames of English verbs and their associated semantic roles.

VerbNet arguments are specified in terms of syntactic categories with associated selectional restrictions, which we translate into regular expressions over relations resulting from our UD translations – basically syntactic roles or prepositions. Figure 3 shows our translations of some of the frames that VerbNet version 3.3 specifies for the verb *look*.

To choose the VerbNet frame to use, we pick the frame that has the fewest items not present in the DRS; if there is a tie, we reject all frames that do not specify core relations (`nsubj`, `csubj`, `obj`, `iobj`, `xcomp`, `ccomp`) that are present in the DRS, and pick the remaining one that has the fewest relations in the DRS not present in the frame; and if it still not unique, we keep both options. Notice that we minimize elements in the frame not present in the DRS before the opposite, because the DRS will in many cases contain adjunct relations that are not specified by VerbNet frames.

As an example, consider the sentence *How do people look at and experience art?*. In our translated DRS, the looking event bears three relations: an `nsubj` relation (to the discourse referent of *people*), an `at` relation (to the discourse referent introduced by *art*), and a `how` relation (to some discourse referent (a state) whose identity is asked for). Of the frames in Figure 3, we choose the second one, because it specifies two elements that are both present in the DRS, whereas the other two frames contain elements that are not in the DRS. None of the frames tell us anything about the `how` relation, which should ideally be spelled out as Manner, so this must be resolved in a different way.

5 Comparison with the PMB

In order to assess how well our rule-based system performs, we conducted some experiments comparing our outputs to the German, English, Italian, and Dutch gold standard datasets (produced and checked by human annotators) provided by the Parallel Meaning Bank v. 4.0.0 (Abzianidze et al., 2017). We compare the pipeline output with the test sets of these languages using the Counter tool (van Noord, 2022), which enables the comparison of two DRSs that are expressed in a machine-friendly format called 'clause notation' (see Liu et al. 2021 for details about this notation). We use the automatic parser Stanza (version 1.4.0: Qi et al., 2020) to produce the Universal Dependencies representations which serve as input to our pipeline.

In the clause notation, lexical concepts are referred to via their WordNet synset (Fellbaum, 1998); e.g. the concept expressed by the lemma *man* might be represented as 'man "n.01"'. At present, our pipeline does not deal in this level of lexical granularity, instead simply outputting lemmas as DRS conditions. For the purpose of comparison, we therefore assign all lexical concepts a default WordNet sense, suffixing all such conditions with "n.01".

Our first consideration is coverage. There are a number of cases where the pipeline fails to produce a DRS for a given sentence, and therefore comparison with the PMB would be unilluminating. There are three main causes:

'(csubj|nsubj)': 'Agent', 'over': 'Location', 'through': 'Location', 'into': 'Location'
'(csubj|nsubj)': 'Agent', 'PREP': 'Theme'
'(csubj|nsubj)': 'Agent', 'PREP': 'Location', 'for': 'Theme'

Figure 3: Select translated VerbNet frames for *look*

1. Faulty input: sometimes Stanza fails to produce a sensible input for the pipeline. For example, Stanza sometimes incorrectly interprets '`.`' in German ordinal number expressions as the end of a sentence, and therefore produces inappropriate and often ungrammatical parses.

2. Computation takes too long for a sentence: in case running the linear logic proof takes too much time, we automatically stop the computation after 10 minutes for that sentence. This could merely be a question of optimisation, or might point to issues with certain interactions of our rules.

3. Genuine lack of coverage: our system is still a work in progress, and there are several linguistic phenomena which we do not even attempt to cover at present. One large omission is negation, for instance. Sometimes these gaps merely lead to inaccurate DRSs, but sometimes they make it impossible to derive a complete DRS at all. Although this points to areas where more work is required, failure in these cases does not tell us anything about the accuracy or usefulness of what we *have* implemented.

For this reason, we omit from our comparisons those sentences where we fail to produce a DRS. Coverage ranges from 79–93% – see Table 1.

Table 1 also shows the results of comparison between the output of our pipeline and the PMB gold data. Where we compare our output directly with the gold data (the 'raw' comparison condition), two things are clear: the scores for English are much better than for the other languages, and all four sets of scores are not particularly impressive. This is shown more perspicuously in Figure 4. Why should this be the case?

There are two main reasons for the discrepancy between the English and non-English scores. Firstly, the PMB uses English synsets for all languages, whereas our pipeline uses lemmas for the equivalent conditions, and these are not translated

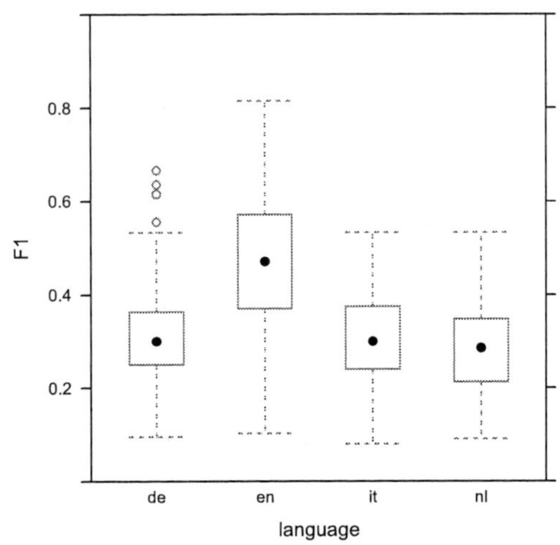

Figure 4: Raw F1 scores across languages

(e.g. where an Italian text uses *uomo*, we will produce a DRS condition 'uomo "n.01"', whereas the PMB gold will have 'man "n.01"'). This means that we will systematically score worse in non-English languages, since almost every single condition which comes from a lexical concept will differ from the PMB gold, and so be scored down in comparison. Secondly, we have only implemented the semantic role labeling step described in Section 4 for English, so once again the non-English languages contain a number of systematic errors: all relations between discourse referents will be wrong since they will have syntactic rather than semantic labels.

The English scores, though, are still not particularly impressive. However, there are a number of things being compared here which we make no effort to cover, and so are bound to do badly on. For instance, we make no effort to find the correct synset for lexical concepts.

Since our focus is on obtaining the correct semantic *structure*, a more illuminating comparison would be to compare the structures of our DRSs, ignoring specific role or concept labels. This was achieved using Counter's `-dr` (default role), `-dc` (default concept), and `-dse` (default word sense)

Language	Raw comparison F1	Rec	Prec	Structural only F1	Rec	Prec	Covered sentences	Total sentences	Proportion covered
German (de)	30.78	30.85	31.21	59.58	57.39	63.48	434	547	0.79
English (en)	46.69	48.07	46.28	63.42	63.92	64.32	874	1048	0.83
Italian (it)	30.68	30.55	31.40	58.88	57.25	61.92	429	461	0.93
Dutch (nl)	28.63	29.07	28.84	58.41	56.84	61.59	399	491	0.81

Table 1: Average F1, Recall, and Precision percentage scores for the sentences covered by our pipeline in the raw and structural-only comparison conditions, followed by number of sentences receiving an analysis, total number of sentences in the dataset, and the corresponding proportion of sentences covered

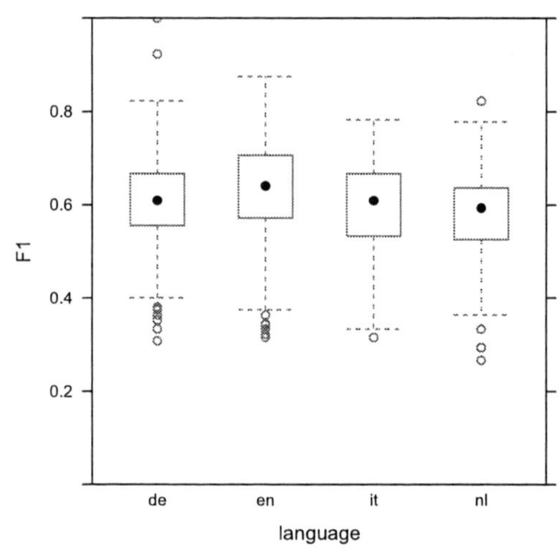

Figure 5: Structural comparison F1 scores across languages

flags, which overall ignores the effect of getting role, concept, or word sense/synset labels incorrect. This enables us to compare DRSs in purely structural terms (along with non-language-specific, discourse-related conditions like PRESUPPOSITION), without worrying about the content of the relations or lexical concepts introduced. F1 scores for this comparison are shown in the second part of Table 1 and visually in Figure 5.

In this setting, the stark difference between English and the other languages disappears, and the scores improve markedly. Some of the higher individual sentence scores are very good, but the averages are dragged down by some very poor scores as well. We anticipate that as the coverage of the rules is expanded, the number of such poorly scoring sentences will diminish, and the overall scores will correspondingly improve.

Our pipeline still performs slightly better on English even in this structural-only setting, which is likely due to the fact that we have so far used English as our primary test language during development of the rules. On the positive side, the fact that performance is quite even across the other three languages, and not much lower than English, shows that our system generalises nicely outside of English. However, it would of course be nice to have gold data from less typologically similar languages to test this further.

Previous work on DRS parsing with neural methods has reported F1 scores in the high 80s on the PMB data (see van Noord et al. 2020). The results of our rule-based pipeline may seem abysmal in comparison, therefore. However, further testing has shown that the rule-based system degrades less as sentence length increases, and may therefore be more robust. Most sentences in the PMB test set are very short: the vast majority are shorter than ten tokens, and the average length is 6.7. To test performance on longer sentences, we annotated Wikipedia text from the GUM corpus (Zeldes, 2017) with the PMB tool. The average sentence length in this dataset is 19.5 tokens. Taking into consideration only data for which a non-zero F1 score is obtained (around 80% of the data for the DL models, and around 60% for our pipeline), Figure 6 shows the F1 scores for our pipeline with gold UD (ud), our pipeline with automatically-generated UD (stanza), a neural parser with no pre-training (no-pt), and a neural parser with the pre-trained bert_base_cased (bert_cased) language model.[4] The neural approaches suffer a major drop in performance compared with the PMB data, while our system suffers a less pronounced degradation. We believe this gives us reason to believe that as our

[4]Here, the no-pre-training and pre-trained models are sequence-to-sequence (seq2seq) models based on common practices for this type of task (cf. Zoph et al., 2016; van Noord et al., 2020; Gheini et al., 2021). The encoder side of the seq2seq model is either a no-pre-training model to be trained or a pre-trained (frozen) model such as bert_base_cased.

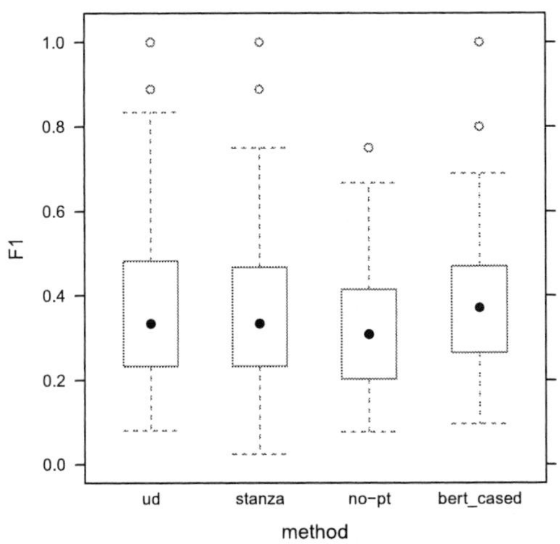

Figure 6: Performance on covered data in GUM corpus

system's rule coverage is improved, performance on both datasets will improve commensurably.

6 Going beyond the PMB

Along with improving our rule coverage to bring us more closely in line with the PMB, there are other areas where we intend to go beyond the PMB and capture additional phenomena via further post-processing steps.

Presupposition is one such area: at present, the DRSs included in the PMB are in the format of Projective Discourse Representation Theory (PDRT: Venhuizen et al., 2013, 2018), and so in principle have access to a rich set of tools for handling the similarities and differences between the information status of various types of projective content such as presupposition, anaphora, and conventional implicature. Setting anaphora to one side for the moment, the projective content the PMB currently contains consists of presuppositions triggered by proper names, definite descriptions, pronouns, and possessives (Abzianidze et al., 2019). Our pipeline also currently captures these, since their triggering contexts are legible in the UD parse (assuming suitable part of speech tags and lexical features). We are currently conducting experimental work to determine other presupposition triggers which can be incorporated into our pipeline, some perhaps on a language-specific basis. The lack of more presuppositional content in the PMB means it does not at present live up to the potential afforded by its PDRT underpinnings.

Anaphora resolution is an essential step in semantic interpretation, which not only changes the labelling of a DRS, but also affects its structure. We do not currently implement any anaphora resolution, whereas the PMB does, so it may be that this is another area where our scores have been dragged down. However, since the PMB dataset consists of fairly short sentences, there will be fewer opportunities for this to make a significant difference. What is more, the PMB's anaphora resolution is apparently fairly unsophisticated, and linguistically naïve: for example, it violates well-established constraints on binding, as in this Principle B violation from the English test data: *Tom*$_i$ *never spoke of him*$_i$. A more robust anaphora resolution system would therefore improve the performance of our pipeline beyond the level of the PMB.

7 Conclusion

We have presented a pipeline for converting Universal Dependencies parses into semantic representations in the form of DRSs. Our rule-based system is intended to provide as linguistically broad a coverage as possible, producing semantic structures which faithfully capture the relations between discourse referents encoded in syntactic structure. Sometimes the UD parse itself is the cause of friction, and we have suggested some ways in which the UD framework might be improved so as to reduce the difficulty of semantic interpretation. Since our rule system produces underspecified DRSs, we also discussed one example post-processing step used to enhance and fully specify our representations. Comparison with the PMB shows that in terms of raw coverage we still have a way to go, but that our goal of capturing universal structural information is on the right track, insofar as our rules seem to generalise across the four languages represented in the PMB to similar extents. Since we now have a successfully implemented system and a working framework for evaluation, we have laid the groundwork for further progress to be made on a theoretical level with regard to improving and expanding the coverage of our ruleset.

Acknowledgements

This research was funded by the Norwegian Research Council, project 300495 *Universal Natural Language Understanding*.

References

Lasha Abzianidze, Johannes Bjerva, Kilian Evang, Hessel Haagsma, Rik van Noord, Pierre Ludmann, Duc-Duy Nguyen, and Johan Bos. 2017. The Parallel Meaning Bank: Towards a multilingual corpus of translations annotated with compositional meaning representations. In *Proceedings of the 15th Conference of the European Chapter of the Association for Computational Linguistics: Volume 2, Short Papers*, pages 242–247, Valencia, Spain. Association for Computational Linguistics.

Lasha Abzianidze, Rik van Noord, Hessel Haagsma, and Johan Bos. 2019. The first shared task on discourse representation structure parsing. In *Proceedings of the IWCS Shared Task on Semantic Parsing*. Association for Computational Linguistics.

Ash Asudeh. 2022. Glue Semantics. *Annual Review of Linguistics*, 8:321–341.

Gosse Bouma, Djamé Seddah, and Daniel Zeman. 2020. Overview of the IWPT 2020 shared task on parsing into enhanced Universal Dependencies. In *Proceedings of the 16th International Conference on Parsing Technologies and the IWPT 2020 Shared Task on Parsing into Enhanced Universal Dependencies*, pages 151–161, Online. Association for Computational Linguistics.

Lucas Champollion. 2015. The interaction of compositional semantics and event semantics. *Linguistics and Philosophy*, 38(1):31–66.

Haskell B. Curry and Robert Feys. 1958. *Combinatory logic: volume I*. North Holland, Amsterdam.

Mary Dalrymple, John Lamping, and Vijay Saraswat. 1993. LFG semantics via constraints. In Steven Krauwer, Michael Moortgat, and Louis des Tombe, editors, *Proceedings of the Sixth Conference of the European Chapter of the Association for Computational Linguistics (EACL 1993)*, pages 97–105.

Donald Davidson. 1967. The logical form of action sentences. In Nicholas Rescher, editor, *The Logic of Decision and Action*, pages 81–120. University of Pittsburgh Press, Pittsburgh, PA.

Christiane Fellbaum, editor. 1998. *WordNet: an electronic lexical database*. MIT Press, Cambridge, MA.

Jamie Y. Findlay and Dag T. T. Haug. 2021. How useful are enhanced Universal Dependencies for semantic interpretation? In *Proceedings of the Sixth International Conference on Dependency Linguistics (Depling, SyntaxFest 2021)*, pages 22–34, Sofia, Bulgaria. Association for Computational Linguistics.

Dan Garrette and Ewan Klein. 2009. An extensible toolkit for computational semantics. In *Proceedings of the Eight International Conference on Computational Semantics*, pages 116–127, Tilburg, The Netherlands. Association for Computational Linguistics.

Mozhdeh Gheini, Xiang Ren, and Jonathan May. 2021. Cross-attention is all you need: Adapting pretrained Transformers for machine translation. In *Proceedings of the 2021 Conference on Empirical Methods in Natural Language Processing*, pages 1754–1765, Online and Punta Cana, Dominican Republic. Association for Computational Linguistics.

Jean-Yves Girard. 1987. Linear logic. *Theoretical Computer Science*, 50(1):1–102.

Matthew Gotham and Dag T. T. Haug. 2018. Glue semantics for Universal Dependencies. In Miriam Butt and Tracy Holloway King, editors, *Proceedings of the LFG'18 Conference*, pages 208–226. CSLI Publications, Stanford, CA.

Barry Haddow, Rachel Bawden, Antonio Valerio Miceli Barone, Jindřich Helcl, and Alexandra Birch. 2022. Survey of low-resource machine translation. *Computational Linguistics*, 48(3):673–732.

Dag T. T. Haug and Jamie Y. Findlay. 2023. Formal semantics for Dependency Grammar. In *Proceedings of the Seventh International Conference on Dependency Linguistics (Depling 2023)*. Association for Computational Linguistics.

William A. Howard. 1980. The formulae-as-types notion of construction. In *To H. B. Curry: essays on combinatory logic, lambda calculus, and formalism*, pages 479–490. Academic Press, London. Circulated in unpublished form from 1969.

Hai Hu, Qi Chen, Kyle Richardson, Atreyee Mukherjee, Lawrence S. Moss, and Sandra Kuebler. 2020. MonaLog: a lightweight system for natural language inference based on monotonicity. In *Proceedings of the Society for Computation in Linguistics 2020*, pages 334–344, New York, New York. Association for Computational Linguistics.

Aikaterini-Lida Kalouli and Richard Crouch. 2018. GKR: the graphical knowledge representation for semantic parsing. In *Proceedings of the Workshop on Computational Semantics beyond Events and Roles*, pages 27–37, New Orleans, Louisiana. Association for Computational Linguistics.

Hans Kamp and Uwe Reyle. 1993. *From discourse to logic*. Kluwer, Dordrecht.

Hans Kamp, Josef van Genabith, and Uwe Reyle. 2011. Discourse Representation Theory. In Dov M. Gabbay and Franz Guenthner, editors, *Handbook of philosophical logic*, 2nd edition, volume 15, pages 125–394. Springer, Berlin.

Karin Kipper, Anna Korhonen, Neville Ryant, and Martha Palmer. 2008. A large-scale classification of English verbs. *Language Resources and Evaluation*, 42(1):21–40.

Jiangming Liu, Shay B. Cohen, Mirella Lapata, and Johan Bos. 2021. Universal discourse representation structure parsing. *Computational Linguistics*, 47(2):445–476.

Moritz Messmer and Mark-Matthias Zymla. 2018. The Glue Semantics Workbench: a modular toolkit for exploring linear logic and Glue Semantics. In *Proceedings of the LFG'18 Conference*, pages 249–263, Stanford, CA. CSLI Publications.

Joakim Nivre, Marie-Catherine de Marneffe, Filip Ginter, Jan Hajič, Christopher D. Manning, Sampo Pyysalo, Sebastian Schuster, Francis Tyers, and Daniel Zeman. 2020. Universal Dependencies v2: An evergrowing multilingual treebank collection. In *Proceedings of the 12th Language Resources and Evaluation Conference*, pages 4034–4043, Marseille, France. European Language Resources Association.

Joakim Nivre, Paola Marongiu, Filip Ginter, Jenna Kanerva, Simonetta Montemagni, Sebastian Schuster, and Maria Simi. 2018. Enhancing Universal Dependency treebanks: A case study. In *Proceedings of the Second Workshop on Universal Dependencies (UDW 2018)*, pages 102–107, Brussels, Belgium. Association for Computational Linguistics.

Jenna Nyblom, Samuel Kohonen, Katri Haverinen, Tapio Salakoski, and Filip Ginter. 2013. Predicting conjunct propagation and other extended Stanford dependencies. In *Proceedings of the Second International Conference on Dependency Linguistics (DepLing 2013)*, pages 252–261, Prague, Czech Republic. Charles University in Prague, Matfyzpress, Prague, Czech Republic.

Terence Parsons. 1990. *Events in the semantics of English: a study in subatomic semantics*. MIT Press, Cambridge, MA.

Agnieszka Patejuk and Adam Przepiórkowski. 2018. *From Lexical Functional Grammar to Enhanced Universal Dependencies: linguistically informed treebanks of Polish*. Institute of Computer Science Polish Academy of Sciences, Warsaw.

Adam Przepiórkowski and Agnieszka Patejuk. 2018. Arguments and adjuncts in Universal Dependencies. In *Proceedings of the 27th International Conference on Computational Linguistics*, pages 3837–3852, Santa Fe, New Mexico, USA. Association for Computational Linguistics.

Adam Przepiórkowski and Agnieszka Patejuk. 2020. From Lexical Functional Grammar to enhanced Universal Dependencies: the UD-LFG treebank of Polish. *Language Resources and Evaluation*, 54(1):185–221.

Peng Qi, Yuhao Zhang, Yuhui Zhang, Jason Bolton, and Christopher D. Manning. 2020. Stanza: A Python natural language processing toolkit for many human languages. In *Proceedings of the 58th Annual Meeting of the Association for Computational Linguistics: System Demonstrations*.

Sebastian Schuster and Christopher D. Manning. 2016. Enhanced English Universal Dependencies: An improved representation for natural language understanding tasks. In *Proceedings of the Tenth International Conference on Language Resources and Evaluation (LREC'16)*, pages 2371–2378, Portorož, Slovenia. European Language Resources Association (ELRA).

Rik van Noord. 2022. Rikvn/drs_parsing: Scripts to evaluate scoped meaning representations. `https://github.com/RikVN/DRS_parsing`. Accessed: 2022-07-19.

Rik van Noord, Antonio Toral, and Johan Bos. 2020. Character-level representations improve DRS-based semantic parsing even in the age of BERT. In *Proceedings of the 2020 Conference on Empirical Methods in Natural Language Processing (EMNLP)*, pages 4587–4603, Online. Association for Computational Linguistics.

Noortje J. Venhuizen, Johan Bos, and Harm Brouwer. 2013. Parsimonious semantic representations with projection pointers. In *Proceedings of the 10th International Conference on Computational Semantics (IWCS 2013) – Long Papers*, pages 252–263, Potsdam, Germany. Association for Computational Linguistics.

Noortje J. Venhuizen, Johan Bos, Petra Hendriks, and Harm Brouwer. 2018. Discourse semantics with information structure. *Journal of Semantics*, 35(1):127–169.

Amir Zeldes. 2017. The GUM corpus: Creating multilayer resources in the classroom. *Language Resources and Evaluation*, 51(3):581–612.

Barret Zoph, Deniz Yuret, Jonathan May, and Kevin Knight. 2016. Transfer learning for low-resource neural machine translation. In *Proceedings of the 2016 Conference on Empirical Methods in Natural Language Processing*, pages 1568–1575, Austin, Texas. Association for Computational Linguistics.

Are UD Treebanks Getting More Consistent? A Report Card for English UD

Amir Zeldes
Georgetown University
amir.zeldes@georgetown.edu

Nathan Schneider
Georgetown University
nathan.schneider@georgetown.edu

Abstract

Recent efforts to consolidate guidelines and treebanks in the Universal Dependencies project raise the expectation that joint training and dataset comparison is increasingly possible for high-resource languages such as English, which have multiple corpora. Focusing on the two largest UD English treebanks, we examine progress in data consolidation and answer several questions: Are UD English treebanks becoming more internally consistent? Are they becoming more like each other and to what extent? Is joint training a good idea, and if so, since which UD version? Our results indicate that while consolidation has made progress, joint models may still suffer from inconsistencies, which hamper their ability to leverage a larger pool of training data.

1 Introduction

The Universal Dependencies project[1] (de Marneffe et al., 2021) has grown over the past few years to encompass not only over 100 languages, but also over 200 treebanks, meaning several languages now have multiple treebanks with rich morphosyntactic and other annotations. Multiple treebanks are especially common for high resource languages such as English, which currently has data in 9 different repositories, totaling over 762,000 tokens (as of UD v2.11). While this abundance of resources is of course positive, it opens questions about consistency across multiple UD treebanks of the same language, with both theoretical questions about annotation guidelines, and practical ones about the value of joint training on multiple datasets for parsing and other NLP applications.

In this paper we focus on the two largest UD treebanks of English: the English Web Treebank (EWT, Silveira et al. 2014) and the Georgetown University Multilayer corpus (GUM, Zeldes 2017).[2] Although both datasets are meant to follow UD guidelines, their origins are very different: EWT was converted to UD from an older constituent treebank (Bies et al., 2012) into Stanford Dependencies (de Marneffe et al., 2006) and then into UD, while GUM was natively annotated in Stanford Dependencies until 2018, then converted to UD (Peng and Zeldes, 2018), with more material added subsequently via native UD annotation. Coupled with gradual changes and clarifications to the guidelines, there are reasons to expect systematic dataset differences, which UD maintainers (including the authors) have sought to consolidate from UD version to version.

Despite potential pitfalls, NLP tools are increasingly merging UD datasets for joint training: for example, Stanford's popular Stanza toolkit (Qi et al., 2020) defaults to using a model called `combined` for English tagging and parsing, which is trained on EWT and GUM (including the Reddit subset of GUM).[3] We therefore consider it timely to ask whether even the largest, most actively developed UD treebanks for English are actually compatible; if not, to what extent, and are they inching closer together or drifting apart from version to version? Regardless of the answer to these questions, is it a good idea to train jointly on EWT and GUM, and if so, given constant revisions to the data, since what UD version?

2 Related work

Much previous work on consistency in UD has focused on cross-linguistic comparison, and especially on finding likely errors. Some papers have taken a 'breadth-first' automatic approach to identifying any inconsistencies (de Marneffe et al., 2017), with the caveat that many types of differences are hard to detect. Others have taken a more focused approach to particular phenomena,

[1] `https://universaldependencies.org`

[2] Due to licensing, GUM Reddit data (Behzad and Zeldes, 2020) has a separate repo, but we merge both repos below.

[3] Though we focus on English here, the same is true for other UD languages with multiple datasets.

Proceedings of the Sixth Workshop on Universal Dependencies (UDW, GURT/SyntaxFest 2023), pages 58 - 64
March 9-12, 2023

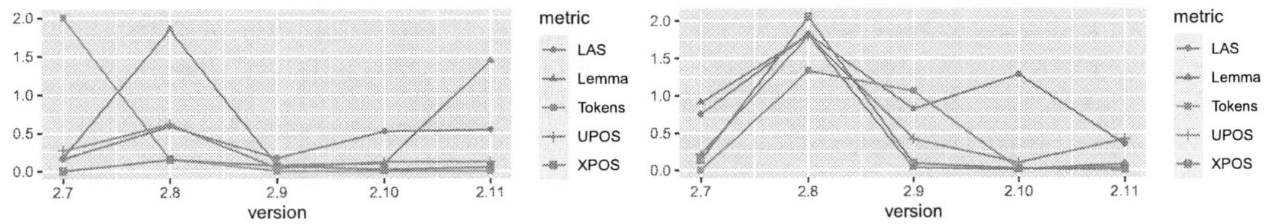

(a) EWT

(b) GUM

Figure 1: Version-to-version changes across annotation layers in EWT and GUM. Y-values are percentages.

for example Bouma et al. (2018) showed that the `expl` relation was used differently across languages for comparable cases, using UD v2.1. Sanguinetti et al. (2022) show a broad range of practices in annotating user-generated content from the Web across UD languages in v2.6. Dönicke et al. (2020) also showed inconsistencies within UD languages using UD v2.5, including the finding that two of the top 20 most inconsistently headed relations in UD came from English, where across 7 datasets, `compound` and `csubj` behaved differently (of these, only the latter differed substantially in EWT and GUM, though the authors write it is possible that GUM 'simply contains more sentences with expletives'). Aggarwal and Zeman (2020) examined part of speech (POS) tag consistency in UD v2.5 and found that POS was relatively internally consistent within most languages.

Fewer studies have examined cross-corpus parsing accuracy (Alonso and Zeman 2016 for Spanish on UD v1.3, Droganova et al. 2018 for Russian using UD v2.2), and fewer still have looked at parsing consistency and stability (Kalpakchi and Boye, 2021). However to the best of our knowledge, no previous study has examined changes in consistency across UD versions, i.e. whether cross-treebank compatibility is increasing over time, how much so, and for which annotations?

3 How has the data changed?

To see how data in both corpora has changed across versions, we use the official CoNLL 2018 UD Shared Task (Zeman et al., 2018) scorer and compare each of the past six versions of each corpus to its next version, taking the updated version as an improved 'gold' standard.[4] This results in a score for each UD metric, such as the labeled attachment score (LAS), universal POS (UPOS) and English-specific POS (XPOS), as well as lemmatization and tokenization. Figure 1 shows the difference in score between each pair of versions for each dataset, which we discuss for each corpus below. For example, taking v2.7 of EWT as the correction for v2.6, we see a 2% rate of tokenization errors (in green), indicating a substantial change in tokenization, but less than 0.2% change to v2.8, and zero changes to tokenization moving to v2.9.

One caveat to note when working with data across versions is that unlike EWT, GUM's contents are not frozen: the corpus grows with new material every year. In the overview below, we therefore keep the evaluation fixed and limited only to documents that have existed since v2.6 (136 documents, 120K tokens). In §4 we will consider scenarios using both this fixed subset and the entire corpus (193 documents, 180K tokens in v2.11).[5]

3.1 EWT

Below we explain the main causes of the larger differentials between consecutive versions.

Tokenization Multiword tokens (MWTs) were added for most clitics (e.g. *'ll*) and contractions (*don't*) in v2.7, with some stragglers in v2.8. Essentially no changes to tokenization were made in subsequent versions.

Tagging Moderate UPOS changes occurred in 2.7 (many WH-words changed to `SCONJ`) and 2.8 (`ADJ` and `VERB` for adjectives and verbs in proper names, formerly `PROPN`, paralleling the XPOS `NNP`); this change was followed by GUM as well, see below. XPOS changes were small, peaking in 2.8 for select expressions like *of course*, *at least*, and *United States*.

Lemmatization Lemma errors were corrected throughout, but principal sources of lemma changes in v2.8 included capitalization of the content word lemmas in proper names, the lemma for the pronoun *I*, and removal of comparative or superlative

[4]Earlier comparisons are impossible since they predate GUM's conversion to UD.

[5]The subsequent release of the larger GUM v9, with 203K tokens and 213 documents, was around the same time as the camera-ready deadline for this paper, and could not be evaluated in time.

degree in the lemmas of *better* and *best*. In v2.11, a new policy for possessive pronoun lemmas was enacted to remove a key discrepancy with GUM.

Dependencies As shown in Figure 1a, the largest changes to LAS occurred in versions 2.8, when newly tagged `ADJ` tokens in names triggered `amod`; 2.10, where the analysis of the *X, so Y* construction was changed to `parataxis` (among others); and 2.11, which featured changes to nesting subjects (`nsubj:outer`), relative constructions, and clefts.

3.2 GUM

Similarly to EWT, GUM has become more stable across layers, with little change to XPOS or lemmas since v2.9. However earlier versions show several substantial revisions. Many changes are again simply due to error corrections, but some systematic changes include the following.

Tokenization saw major changes in v2.8, with the introduction of MWTs to match EWT changes. Additional major changes in v2.9 resulted from changing word tokenization to match EWT and other recent LDC corpora, which tokenize hyphenated compounds (e.g. v2.7 has *data-driven* as one token, but v2.8 has three tokens, like EWT).

Tagging shows a similar shift in v2.8 due to introduction of the `HYPH` tag for hyphens in compounds like 'data-driven', but also the removal of special XPOS tags for square brackets (`-LSB-` and `-RSB-` for left/right square brackets were collapsed with the round bracket tags `-LRB-/-RRB-`, again matching EWT). Changes to UPOS, by contrast, are more substantial, primarily due to verbs/adjectives in proper names, as in EWT above. Later changes to UPOS in v2.9 and 2.11 result from retagging some pronominal determiners (XPOS `DT`) as `DET` and not `PRON` (*some, all, both*), and changing WH subordinators from `SCONJ` to `ADV` respectively, again in harmony with changes to EWT.

Lemmatization largely reflects the hyphenation change (since e.g. 'data-driven' is no longer a lemma in v2.8) and the change from `PROPN` to `VERB` or `ADJ` in names, since the lemma for '*Glowing*' in '*the Glowing Sea*' was changed from '*Glowing*' (based on being `PROPN`) to '*Glow*' (as a `VERB`).

Dependencies Here too, transition to new tokenization and tagging names created changes in v2.8, but we also see a peak in v2.10, primarily due to consolidation of proper name dependencies (changing `flat` to syntactically transparent analyses), more aggressive identification of ellipsis (with promoted arguments) and `orphan` relations, and removal of some uses of the `dep` relation.

4 Cross-corpus parsing

Cross-corpus results To test whether EWT and GUM are becoming more internally and mutually consistent, we train parsers on each version of each corpus, and test them against both corpora. If each corpus is becoming more consistent, we expect higher scores in each version; and if cross-corpus model scores are increasing, we infer that the data is becoming more consistent across corpora. To ensure a fair comparison, we keep training and test data from GUM fixed to those documents that have been available since v2.6.

The results in Table 1 show that within-corpus scores are indeed improving slightly with each version (all scores are 3-run averages using Diaparser, Attardi et al. 2021, a recent transformer-based biaffine dependency parser). Cross-corpus scores are substantially lower, but also improving: in v2.6, EWT in-domain LAS was 90.24, which has improved slightly to 90.9 in v2.11, but scores training on GUM and testing on EWT have gone up from 81.78 to 84.27. In the opposite direction, GUM in-domain scores improved from LAS=87.9 to 89.48, or for a parser trained on EWT, from 83.89 to 84.74. The macro-average of both corpora also shows a steady increase, more so on GUM. In all cases, v2.11 is the best version yet for all metrics.

However, since the experiments are limited to the smaller subset of UD GUM v2.6 documents, they do not reflect current NLP tools (which train on all documents in the current UD repos), nor do they tell us whether joint training is a good idea.

Joint training results In this series of experiments we train on both corpora jointly, comparing two scenarios: the SUBSET scenario limits GUM training data to the v2.6 subset, while ALL uses all available GUM documents for training at each version; for fairness, scores are always limited to documents in the v2.6 test set, which are a subset of all subsequent release test sets.[6]

Table 2 shows that here too, there is only improvement over time. Using all GUM documents is superior to just the subset on GUM, but actually leads to a slight degradation on EWT, presumably due to the inclusion of more out-of-domain data

[6] Note that no new documents were added to GUM in v2.7, hence scores are identical for SUBSET and ALL until v2.8.

train	version	EWT test UAS (sd)		EWT test LAS (sd)		GUM test UAS (sd)		GUM test LAS (sd)		Macro-Avg UAS (sd)		Macro-Avg LAS (sd)	
EWT	v2.6	92.82	0.132	90.24	0.066	87.81	0.073	83.89	0.023	90.31	0.059	87.07	0.025
	v2.7	92.84	0.037	90.25	0.173	87.87	0.088	84.19	0.074	90.35	0.062	87.22	0.114
	v2.8	92.93	0.060	90.42	0.090	87.97	0.078	84.90	0.028	90.45	0.065	87.66	0.042
	v2.9	92.88	0.107	90.41	0.131	87.57	0.148	84.36	0.105	90.23	0.098	87.38	0.117
	v2.10	93.06	0.082	90.70	0.158	87.81	0.084	84.72	0.138	90.44	0.082	87.71	0.088
	v2.11	**93.18**	0.142	**90.90**	0.139	**88.05**	0.260	**84.74**	0.289	**90.62**	0.196	**87.82**	0.207
GUM	v2.6	86.53	0.357	81.78	0.397	91.37	0.201	87.90	0.141	88.95	0.187	84.84	0.209
	v2.7	86.69	0.336	82.28	0.322	91.66	0.156	88.24	0.284	89.18	0.242	85.26	0.299
	v2.8	87.02	0.133	82.90	0.214	91.88	0.132	88.86	0.159	89.45	0.002	85.88	0.041
	v2.9	87.42	0.143	83.43	0.025	91.88	0.300	88.78	0.281	89.65	0.219	86.11	0.140
	v2.10	87.53	0.190	83.79	0.191	92.16	0.216	89.24	0.191	89.85	0.203	86.51	0.191
	v2.11	**88.23**	0.198	**84.27**	0.095	**92.28**	0.137	**89.48**	0.224	**90.26**	0.121	**86.88**	0.132

Table 1: Cross-corpus parsing scores (three run averages with standard deviations)

train	version	EWT test UAS (sd)		EWT test LAS (sd)		GUM test UAS (sd)		GUM test LAS (sd)		Macro-Avg UAS (sd)		Macro-Avg LAS (sd)	
JOINT$_{subset}$	v2.6	92.38	0.044	89.59	0.108	90.08	0.366	86.80	0.326	91.23	0.177	88.20	0.146
	v2.7	92.31	0.078	89.61	0.072	90.15	0.311	86.96	0.360	91.23	0.122	88.29	0.148
	v2.8	92.49	0.159	89.99	0.128	90.51	0.351	87.86	0.449	91.50	0.154	88.92	0.195
	v2.9	92.39	0.324	89.80	0.278	90.63	0.392	87.91	0.415	91.51	0.086	88.85	0.114
	v2.10	92.62	0.034	90.24	0.058	90.51	0.418	87.86	0.381	91.56	0.192	89.05	0.163
	v2.11	**92.92**	0.072	**90.58**	0.052	**90.75**	0.073	**87.94**	0.059	**91.83**	0.064	**89.26**	0.045
JOINT$_{all}$	v2.6	92.38	0.044	89.59	0.108	90.08	0.366	86.80	0.326	91.23	0.177	88.20	0.146
	v2.7	92.31	0.078	89.61	0.072	90.15	0.311	86.96	0.360	91.23	0.122	88.29	0.148
	v2.8	92.07	0.277	89.55	0.312	91.26	0.267	88.72	0.247	91.66	0.077	89.14	0.066
	v2.9	92.27	0.154	89.77	0.287	90.81	0.084	88.12	0.123	91.54	0.110	88.95	0.176
	v2.10	92.18	0.018	89.86	0.010	91.54	0.170	88.99	0.211	91.86	0.092	89.43	0.110
	v2.11	**92.54**	0.259	**90.11**	0.240	**91.71**	0.426	**89.11**	0.534	**92.13**	0.147	**89.61**	0.181

Table 2: Joint training parsing scores (three run averages with standard deviations)

from the EWT perspective. Nevertheless, JOINT$_{all}$ performance on EWT also improves over time.

The best in-domain numbers from Table 1 are always better than the best joint training numbers, indicating that the added data cannot quite compensate for the distraction of different genres in each corpus, and possible remaining annotation inconsistencies. This is not surprising given the importance of genre for NLP performance (Zeldes and Simonson, 2016; Müller-Eberstein et al., 2021). In fact, similar tradeoffs of a helpful increase in data size vs. a harmful increase in heterogeneity have been observed for UD parsing in other languages (see Zeldes et al. 2022 for Hebrew, León 2020 for Spanish) and similarly for other tasks (e.g. for discourse parsing, Peng et al. 2022; Liu and Zeldes 2023).

However, the gap is narrowing: the joint model has gained about a point on EWT, placing it only 0.32 points behind the best in-domain model, and it has gained 2.31 points on GUM for the best ALL scenario in v2.11. Perhaps more importantly, the macroaverage, which may better reflect 'real-world' applicability of the parser model to any unseen genre data (since the macro-test set contains the most target genres), is now at LAS=89.61, within one point of the best models for each corpus.

Since the best joint result is also for v2.11, it seems fair to answer the questions posed at the beginning of this paper as follows: it has never been a better idea to train jointly than now; joint training always lags closely behind in-domain training, but the gap has been narrowing and is now very small; and for totally unseen new data, the joint model now looks like a very good idea. The joint SUBSET model is a close second on EWT, and the joint ALL model is the runner-up on GUM. That said, the fact that more data in the form of a second corpus does not outperform in-domain training alone suggests that there are still inconsistencies between the corpora, on which the next UD versions can hopefully improve.

In terms of concerns about what current jointly trained parsers are actually getting wrong, we direct readers to the confusion matrices in Figure 2 in the Appendix, which indicates that despite training on distinct datasets, the most common errors on both test sets are invariably confusing nmod and obl, which usually corresponds to a PP attachment error. Other systematic errors are rare, and largely concern notable subcategories of names and other types of terms. One recurring subtype is GUM's dep label being confused with EWT nummod for numeric modifiers which are not count-modifiers (e.g. 'Page **3**' has '3' as dep in GUM but nummod in EWT; GUM only uses nummod for counting cases like '3 pages'). Several of these discrepancies are discussed in Schneider and Zeldes (2021) and form a target for further consolidation.

Also of possible concern are compound relations, which a GUM-trained model predicts for various gold-standard relations in EWT, and an EWT model predicts for various gold-standard relations in GUM. It seems likely that these are remaining artifacts from the automatic conversion of the EWT gold constituent annotations to dependencies, in which various complex nominals were analyzed as compounds, for example for names such as *Sri Lanka* or *Hong Kong* (right-headed compound in EWT, but left-headed flat in GUM) and borrowed foreign words or phrases such as *cordon-blu* (*sic*) (again right-headed in EWT, would be flat in GUM), or also in complex nested phrases which are analyzed as left branching in EWT, e.g. *Marvel Consultants, Inc.* is headed by *Inc.* with two compound dependents in EWT. In GUM it would be headed by *Consultants* with *Inc.* as acl, or flat for lexicalized cases (attested in GUM for the film *Monsters Inc.*). Similarly, capitalized adjectival modifiers with XPOS NNP are sometimes labeled as compound in EWT, leading to amod predictions in the GUM-trained model and vice versa (e.g. *Islamist officers* or *Baathist saboteurs*).

5 Discussion

In this paper we surveyed progress in consolidating the largest UD English corpora, EWT and GUM. Results show data is moving closer together: single-corpus training still beats joint training by a hair, but joint models are nearly as good, and likely much more robust. As consolidation continues, we hope to see joint models overtake in-domain training, and more consistency expanding to other English datasets and other UD languages.

References

Akshay Aggarwal and Daniel Zeman. 2020. Estimating POS annotation consistency of different treebanks in a language. In *Proceedings of the 19th International Workshop on Treebanks and Linguistic Theories*, pages 93–110, Düsseldorf, Germany. Association for Computational Linguistics.

Héctor Martínez Alonso and Daniel Zeman. 2016. Universal Dependencies for the AnCora treebanks. *Procesamiento del Lenguaje Natural*, 57:91–98.

Giuseppe Attardi, Daniele Sartiano, and Maria Simi. 2021. Biaffine dependency and semantic graph parsing for Enhanced Universal dependencies. In *Proceedings of the 17th International Conference on Parsing Technologies and the IWPT 2021 Shared Task on Parsing into Enhanced Universal Dependencies (IWPT 2021)*, pages 184–188, Online. Association for Computational Linguistics.

Shabnam Behzad and Amir Zeldes. 2020. A cross-genre ensemble approach to robust Reddit part of speech tagging. In *Proceedings of the 12th Web as Corpus Workshop*, pages 50–56, Marseille, France. European Language Resources Association.

Ann Bies, Justin Mott, Colin Warner, and Seth Kulick. 2012. English Web Treebank. Technical Report LDC2012T13, Linguistic Data Consortium, Philadelphia, PA.

Gosse Bouma, Jan Hajic, Dag Haug, Joakim Nivre, Per Erik Solberg, and Lilja Øvrelid. 2018. Expletives in Universal Dependency treebanks. In *Proceedings of the Second Workshop on Universal Dependencies (UDW 2018)*, pages 18–26, Brussels, Belgium. Association for Computational Linguistics.

Marie-Catherine de Marneffe, Matias Grioni, Jenna Kanerva, and Filip Ginter. 2017. Assessing the annotation consistency of the Universal Dependencies corpora. In *Proceedings of the Fourth International Conference on Dependency Linguistics (Depling 2017)*, pages 108–115, Pisa,Italy. Linköping University Electronic Press.

Marie-Catherine de Marneffe, Bill MacCartney, and Christopher D. Manning. 2006. Generating typed dependency parses from phrase structure parses. In *Proceedings of LREC 2006*, pages 449–454, Genoa, Italy.

Marie-Catherine de Marneffe, Christopher D. Manning, Joakim Nivre, and Daniel Zeman. 2021. Universal Dependencies. *Computational Linguistics*, 47(2):255–308.

Tillmann Dönicke, Xiang Yu, and Jonas Kuhn. 2020. Identifying and handling cross-treebank inconsistencies in UD: A pilot study. In *Proceedings of the Fourth Workshop on Universal Dependencies (UDW 2020)*, pages 67–75, Barcelona, Spain (Online). Association for Computational Linguistics.

Kira Droganova, Olga Lyashevskaya, and Daniel Zeman. 2018. Data conversion and consistency of monolingual corpora: Russian UD treebanks. In *Proceedings of the 17th International Workshopon Treebanks and Linguistic Theories (TLT 2018)*, pages 53–66,, Linköping, Sweden. Linköping University Electronic Press.

Dmytro Kalpakchi and Johan Boye. 2021. Minor changes make a difference: a case study on the consistency of UD-based dependency parsers. In *Proceedings of the Fifth Workshop on Universal Dependencies (UDW, SyntaxFest 2021)*, pages 96–108, Sofia, Bulgaria. Association for Computational Linguistics.

Fernando Sánchez León. 2020. Combining different parsers and datasets for CAPITEL UD parsing. In *Proceedings of the Iberian Languages Evaluation Forum (IberLEF 2020) co-located with 36th Conference of the Spanish Society for Natural Language Processing (SEPLN 2020), Málaga, Spain, September 23th, 2020*, volume 2664 of *CEUR Workshop Proceedings*, pages 39–44. CEUR-WS.org.

Yang Janet Liu and Amir Zeldes. 2023. Why can't discourse parsing generalize? A thorough investigation of the impact of data diversity. In *Proceedings of EACL 2023*, Dubrovnik, Croatia.

Max Müller-Eberstein, Rob van der Goot, and Barbara Plank. 2021. Genre as weak supervision for cross-lingual dependency parsing. In *Proceedings of the 2021 Conference on Empirical Methods in Natural Language Processing*, pages 4786–4802, Online and Punta Cana, Dominican Republic. Association for Computational Linguistics.

Siyao Peng, Yang Janet Liu, and Amir Zeldes. 2022. GCDT: A Chinese RST treebank for multigenre and multilingual discourse parsing. In *Proceedings of the 2nd Conference of the Asia-Pacific Chapter of the Association for Computational Linguistics and the 12th International Joint Conference on Natural Language Processing (Volume 2: Short Papers)*, pages 382–391, Online only. Association for Computational Linguistics.

Siyao Peng and Amir Zeldes. 2018. All roads lead to UD: Converting Stanford and Penn parses to English Universal Dependencies with multilayer annotations. In *Proceedings of the Joint Workshop on Linguistic Annotation, Multiword Expressions and Constructions (LAW-MWE-CxG-2018)*, pages 167–177, Santa Fe, NM.

Peng Qi, Yuhao Zhang, Yuhui Zhang, Jason Bolton, and Christopher D. Manning. 2020. Stanza: A Python natural language processing toolkit for many human languages. In *Proceedings of the 58th Annual Meeting of the Association for Computational Linguistics: System Demonstrations*, pages 101–108.

Manuela Sanguinetti, Lauren Cassidy, Cristina Bosco, Özlem Çetinoğlu, Alessandra Teresa Cignarella, Teresa Lynn, Ines Rehbein, Josef Ruppenhofer, Djamé Seddah, and Amir Zeldes. 2022. Treebanking user-generated content: a UD based overview of guidelines, corpora and unified recommendations. *Language Resources and Evaluation*.

Nathan Schneider and Amir Zeldes. 2021. Mischievous nominal constructions in Universal Dependencies. In *Proceedings of the Fifth Workshop on Universal Dependencies (UDW, SyntaxFest 2021)*, pages 160–172, Sofia, Bulgaria. Association for Computational Linguistics.

Natalia Silveira, Timothy Dozat, Marie-Catherine de Marneffe, Samuel Bowman, Miriam Connor, John Bauer, and Christopher D. Manning. 2014. A gold standard dependency corpus for English. In *Proceedings of the Ninth International Conference on Language Resources and Evaluation (LREC-2014)*.

Amir Zeldes. 2017. The GUM corpus: Creating multilayer resources in the classroom. *Language Resources and Evaluation*, 51(3):581–612.

Amir Zeldes, Nick Howell, Noam Ordan, and Yifat Ben Moshe. 2022. A second wave of UD Hebrew treebanking and cross-domain parsing. In *Proceedings of EMNLP 2022*, Abu Dhabi, UAE.

Amir Zeldes and Dan Simonson. 2016. Different flavors of GUM: Evaluating genre and sentence type effects on multilayer corpus annotation quality. In *Proceedings of the 10th Linguistic Annotation Workshop held in conjunction with ACL 2016 (LAW-X 2016)*, pages 68–78, Berlin, Germany. Association for Computational Linguistics.

Daniel Zeman, Jan Hajič, Martin Popel, Martin Potthast, Milan Straka, Filip Ginter, Joakim Nivre, and Slav Petrov. 2018. CoNLL 2018 shared task: Multilingual parsing from raw text to Universal Dependencies. In *Proceedings of the CoNLL 2018 Shared Task: Multilingual Parsing from Raw Text to Universal Dependencies*, pages 1–21, Brussels, Belgium. Association for Computational Linguistics.

A Confusion matrices

Figure 2 gives confusion matrices for dependency relation predictions (disregarding correct/incorrect attachment) for the joint and cross-corpus scenarios, testing on GUM (left) and EWT (right). In all cases, the most frequently confused errors are `obl` and `nmod` in both directions, largely corresponding to PP attachment ambiguity errors (i.e. high attachment to the verb for 'eat a pizza with a fork' versus low attachment to the object noun in 'eat a pizza with anchovies'). These errors are encouraging in that they are unlikely to reflect annotation practice differences between the corpora.

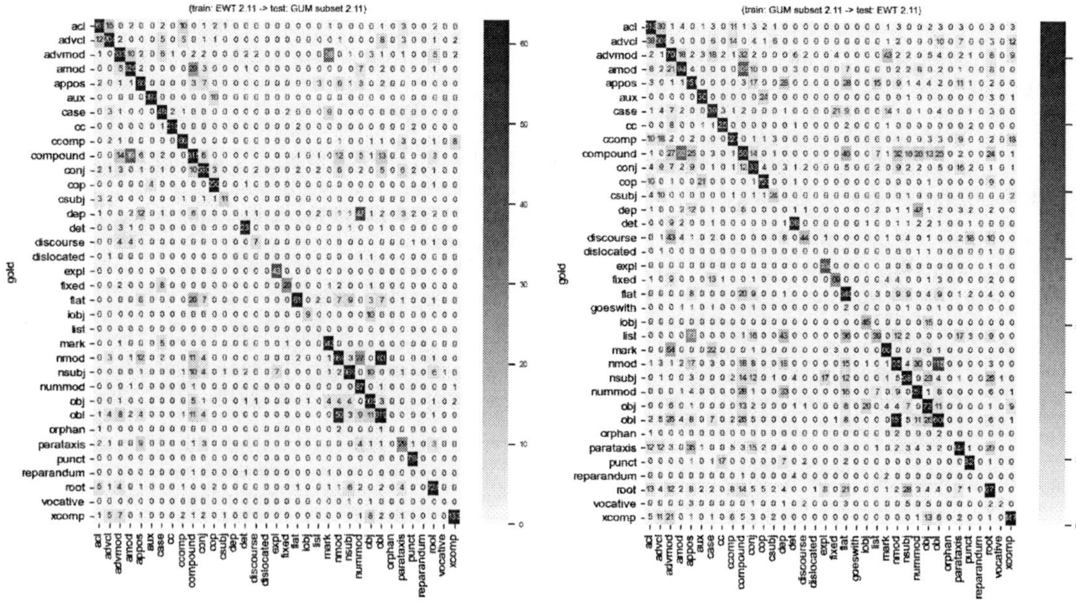

(a) Dependency relation errors for cross-corpus training

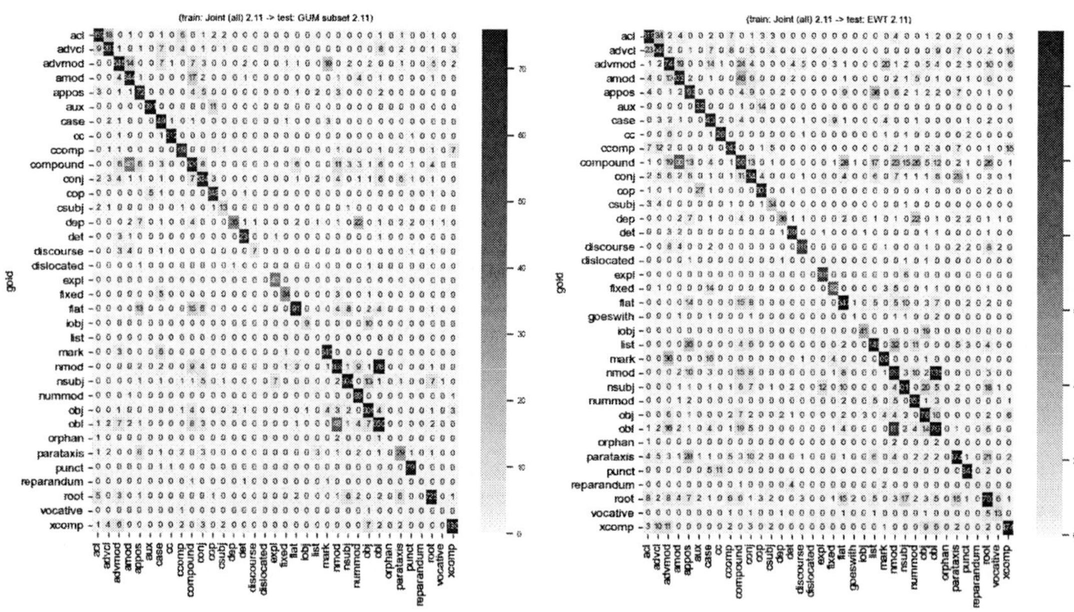

(b) Dependency relation errors for joint training

Figure 2: Confusion matrices for cross-corpus (a) and joint-corpus (b) dependency relation predictions on both test sets, using the GUM v2.6 document subset for GUM and the average performing parser model from each experiment.

Introducing Morphology in Universal Dependencies Japanese

Chihiro Taguchi and **David Chiang**
University of Notre Dame, USA
{ctaguchi,dchiang}@nd.edu

Abstract

This paper discusses the need for including morphological features in Japanese Universal Dependencies (UD). In the current version (v2.11) of the Japanese UD treebanks, sentences are tokenized at the morpheme level, and almost no morphological feature annotation is used. However, Japanese is not an isolating language that lacks morphological inflection but is an agglutinative language. Given this situation, we introduce a tentative scheme for retokenization and morphological feature annotation for Japanese UD. Then, we measure and compare the morphological complexity of Japanese with other languages to demonstrate that the proposed tokenizations show similarities to synthetic languages reflecting the linguistic typology.

1 Introduction

This paper introduces morphology-aware tokenization and morphological features to Universal Dependencies (UD) treebanks for Japanese. Since its inception in 2015, the UD project has been developed to cover more than 130 languages as of v2.11 (de Marneffe et al., 2021; Zeman et al., 2022). Its crosslinguistically consistent syntactic and morphological annotation has enabled corpus-based multilingual NLP at a greater scale (Nivre et al., 2020). However, the Japanese treebanks in the current UD v2.11 have divergent policies in terms of tokenization and morphological feature annotation. Specifically, sentences are tokenized by morpheme boundaries with almost no morphological feature assigned, despite the linguistic fact that Japanese has morphological inflection. Given this issue, this paper will propose new tentative schemes for tokenization and morphological annotation that takes into account the synthetic nature of Japanese. Then, we will demonstrate that the retokenized Japanese UD treebanks with these schemes have morphological complexities similar to other synthetic languages. These results agree with the typology of Japanese as a synthetic agglutinative language.

2 Background

This section overviews the Japanese language and the annotation issues that the current Japanese UD treebanks have. It is a typical head-final language with synthetic morphology, where grammatical information is mostly expressed by means of agglutination.

2.1 Orthography

Modern Japanese orthography uses three writing systems: *hiragana* (ひらがな), *katakana* (カタカナ), and *kanji* (漢字). The first two are phonographic writing systems, where each character represents a mora.[1] *Kanji* is a logographic system borrowed from Chinese, and one character may be associated with more than one pronunciation. These three writing systems are used in a mixed manner, where *kanji* is typically used for content words including Chinese loanwords, *katakana* mainly for non-Sino-Japanese loanwords such as from English, and *hiragana* elsewhere. In addition, Japanese orthography does not mark word boundaries, unlike many other orthographies that use spaces for indicating boundaries. These orthographic conventions give rise to various controversies in terms of tokenization and standardized lemmatization.

2.2 Morphology

While Japanese morphology is primarily agglutinative, there is also a limited degree of fusional morphology, where one inflectional morpheme is

[1]A mora is a prosodic unit. A single mora includes a Consonant–Vowel (CV) pair, a single vowel, syllable-final /n/, the last part of a long vowel, and the first part of a geminate consonant. For example, the word *kittinkauntaa* "countertop" consists of eight morae (*ki-t-ti-n-ka-u-n-ta-a*).

Proceedings of the Sixth Workshop on Universal Dependencies (UDW, GURT/SyntaxFest 2023), pages 65 - 72

FORM	LEMMA	FEATS
irassyara	*irassyaru*	_
nakat	*nai*	Polarity=Neg
ta	*ta*	_
irassyaranakatta	*irassyaru*	Polarity=Neg|Polite=Resp|Tense=Past|VerbForm=Fin

Table 1: Tokenization, lemmatization, and morphological feature description for (1) with a simplified ConLL-U format. The upper three rows represent the style of the current Japanese UD treebank, and the last row represents the style proposed in this paper. Word forms and lemmas are romanized for readers' convenience.

responsible for more than one feature. For example, the single morpheme *irassyara* in sentence (1) has a grammatical feature of respectful politeness as well as the lexical meaning. Tokenization by a chunk that includes all of enclitics and affixes in a token is called 文節 (*bunsetu*; "sentence parts") in Japanese linguistics.

(1) いらっしゃらなかった
irassyara-nakat-ta
come.RESP-NEG-PST
'(The one respected by the speaker) did not come.'

2.3 Universal Dependencies treebanks

In UD v2.11, Japanese is the second largest language, with approximately 2,849k tokens in total. The seemingly large size is a result of the corpora containing two versions with the same sentences and two different tokenization schemes: Short Unit Word (SUW) and Long Unit Word (LUW). Tokens in SUW are the smallest meaningful units, while LUW's tokenization takes into account compound tokens such as compound nouns and light verb constructions.[2] SUW and LUW largely overlap the notion of *tango* (単語; "word") in the Japanese grammar analyzed by Shinkichi Hashimoto, which is generally taught in the Japanese language education in Japan ("Hashimoto Grammar" (HG) henceforth).

Compared to other treebanks in UD, annotation in Japanese UD is unique in three aspects. First, the tokenization splits at the morpheme level (see the upper three rows of Table 1 for example). This stands in clear contrast with other agglutinative languages in UD, where suffixes are commonly included in one token together with the word root, with their morphological functions expressed as features.

Second, morphological features (FEATS) in Japanese UD treebanks are mostly left blank except for very limited cases such as Polarity=Neg. Other morphemes carrying grammatical features are not provided with any information in FEATS; for instance, grammatical information for RESP and PST in the gloss (1) is not specified as features in Japanese UD (see Table 1).

Third, in the architecture of UD, this strictly morpheme-level tokenization in both SUW and LUW faces a crucial problem: the word form cannot be computed from its lemma and features. For example, although the first token in Table 1 *irassyara* is different from its lemma *irassyaru*, the annotation does not tell us why they have different forms. HG calls the first form *mizenkei* (未然形; "irrealis form"), but this form is not responsible for any specific meaning by itself and therefore is not a morphological feature. Therefore, SUW and LUW fail to capture the morphology of Japanese.

3 Related Work

In the NLP literature on Japanese, the term "morphological analysis" has been used to refer to the task of morphological segmentation, given the fact that the Japanese orthography does not explicitly contain word boundaries (Den et al., 2008; Kudo et al., 2004; Neubig et al., 2011). Since there is no solid linguistic criterion to define what a word is, the smallest meaningful unit (i.e., morpheme) is a stable candidate for tokenizing a language with no orthographic word boundary. This tokenization policy is common in Japanese corpora, as is comprehensively defined in the Balanced Corpus of Contemporary Written Japanese (BCCWJ) (Ogura et al., 2011) as SUW and LUW. Existing Japanese morphological analyzers such as MeCab[3] and Sudachi[4] are based on the same policy, and their main concern has chiefly been morpheme-level tokenization and POS tagging while leaving the analysis of morphological features untouched.

[2]For a comprehensive definition and examples, see https://clrd.ninjal.ac.jp/bccwj/en/morphology.html.

[3]http://taku910.github.io/mecab/

[4]https://www.mlab.im.dendai.ac.jp/~yamada/ir/MorphologicalAnalyzer/Sudachi.html

The above-mentioned issues of Japanese UD have already been raised by multiple researchers. Pringle (2016) gives a comprehensive overview of the tokenization of Japanese UD from the viewpoint of general linguistics, concluding that the current tokenization scheme is an artifact of decisions made by the corpora on which the UD Japanese treebanks were based—decisions which UD Japanese should revisit for the sake of the crosslinguistic nature of UD. Murawaki (2019) provides discussion on defining a word in Japanese for UD, and demonstrates that a word (`FORM`) in Japanese UD does not follow UD's general annotation guideline, which states that "morphological features are encoded as properties of words and there is no attempt at segmenting words into morphemes."[5] However, no actual implementation for retokenization has been realized.

This situation in fact prevents Japanese from being included in crosslinguistic studies with UD data. Çöltekin and Rama (2022) investigate various measures of morphological complexity with more than 50 UD treebanks, but they had to exclude Japanese and Korean treebanks because "no linguistically interesting features were marked despite the fact that both languages are morphologically complex."

4 Retokenization

Given the current issues with Japanese UD, this section proposes tentative alternative annotation schemes that take into account synthetic aspects of Japanese morphology.

4.1 Policies

To define a token in Japanese, we prepared two levels of tokenization policies that reflect Japanese morphological inflection differently. At the first level, each verb and its inflectional morphemes are joined into a single token, which is annotated with appropriate features. These morphemes correspond to 助動詞 (*zyodousi*; "auxiliary verbs") in HG's terms as well as in `XPOS` of conventional Japanese UD treebanks (see Table 6 in Appendix for details). The last row of Table 1 shows an example retokenized on this level for sentence (1).

The second level also joins verbs and their inflectional morphemes as at the first level; in addition, each noun and its case markings are joined into a single token, which is annotated with appropriate features. These case markings are called 格助詞 (*kakuzyosi*; case particles) in HG's terms; see Table 7 for details. Most of the other types of particles are treated as independent tokens.

The motivation to treat verbal inflection suffixes and case markings at different levels of tokenization is that the morphosyntactic distribution of case markers is freer than those in other agglutinative languages that consider them as part of their morphology. Although the Japanese case markings are functionally similar to case suffixes, their less synthetic distribution is as independent as enclitics and more detached than suffixes (Miyaoka, 2002). For example, Japanese cases always have regular forms and can be attached to material already containing a clitic, whereas affixal morphology tends to have irregular inflection and more limited morphosyntactic distribution. However, as Haspelmath (2015) pointed out, there have been no crosslinguistically viable criteria that distinguish a clitic from an affix. For this reason, we leave the rigid morphosyntactic treatment of Japanese case-marking on hold and instead prepare two levels of schemes corresponding to both of the treatments. Table 2 illustrates the comparison of SUW, LUW, *bunsetu*, and the proposed tokenization schemes.

4.2 Implementation

Since this paper cannot give a decisive answer as to which level is linguistically more suitable to UD, we implemented retokenizers for both of these policies. The retokenization and feature assignment were done fully automatically with rule-based token rejoining, thanks to the fine-grained `XPOS` annotation in UD Japanese treebanks.[6] We converted the UD_Japanese-GSD and UD_Japanese-GSDLUW treebanks with respect to the two tokenization levels. GSD and GSDLUW are SUW-based and LUW-based treebanks with the same sentences, respectively.

5 Morphological Complexity of Japanese

To confirm the validity of the morphology-aware Japanese UD treebanks, this section reports experiments to measure the morphological complexity of Japanese, which Çöltekin and Rama (2022) could not compare due to the lack of morphological information in current Japanese UD.

[5] `https://universaldependencies.org/u/overview/tokenization.html`

[6] The codes used in the retokenization process are available here: `https://github.com/ctaguchi/ud_ja_standardize`.

SUW	魚 *sakana* fish NOUN	フライ *hurai* fry NOUN	を *wo* ACC ADP	食べ *tabe* eat VERB	た *ta* PST AUX	か *ka* Q PART	も *mo* also ADP	しれ *sire* know VERB	ない *nai* NEG AUX	ペルシャ *perusya* Persia NOUN	猫 *neko* cat NOUN
LUW	魚フライ *sakanahurai* fried_fish NOUN		を *wo* ACC ADP	食べ *tabe* eat VERB	た *ta* PST AUX	かもしれない *kamosirenai* may AUX				ペルシャ猫 *perusyaneko* Persian_cat NOUN	
bunsetu	魚フライを *sakanahuraiwo*			食べたかもしれない *tabetakamosirenai*						ペルシャ猫 *perusyaneko*	
proposal (SUW$_1$)	魚 *sakana* fish NOUN _	フライ *hurai* fry NOUN _	を *wo* ACC ADP _	食べた *tabeta* eat.PST VERB Tense=Past VerbForm=Fin		か *ka* Q PART _	も *mo* also ADP _	しれない *sirenai* know.NEG VERB Polarity=Neg Tense=Pres VerbForm=Fin		ペルシャ *perusya* Persia NOUN _	猫 *neko* cat NOUN _
proposal (SUW$_2$)	魚 *sakana* fish NOUN _	フライを *huraiwo* fry.ACC NOUN Case=Acc		食べた *tabeta* eat.PST VERB Tense=Past VerbForm=Fin		か *ka* Q PART _	も *mo* also ADP _	しれない *sirenai* know.NEG VERB Polarity=Neg Tense=Pres VerbForm=Fin		ペルシャ *perusya* Persia NOUN _	猫 *neko* cat NOUN _
proposal (LUW$_1$)	魚フライ *sakanahurai* fried_fish NOUN _		を *wo* ACC ADP _	食べた *tabeta* eat.PST VERB Tense=Past VerbForm=Fin		かもしれない *kamosirenai* may AUX Tense=Pres VerbForm=Fin				ペルシャ猫 *perusyaneko* Persian_cat NOUN _	
proposal (LUW$_2$)	魚フライを *sakanahuraiwo* fried_fish.ACC NOUN Case=Acc			食べた *tabeta* eat.PST VERB Tense=Past VerbForm=Fin		かもしれない *kamosirenai* may AUX Tense=Pres VerbForm=Fin				ペルシャ猫 *perusyaneko* Persian_cat NOUN _	

Table 2: Example of different tokenization schemes (SUW, LUW, bunsetu, and the proposed tokenization) for the sentence 魚フライを食べたかもしれないペルシャ猫 ("A Persian cat that might have eaten fried fish") (Omura and Asahara, 2018). Subscripts on SUW and LUW denote the levels of retokenization proposed in this paper.

5.1 Setup

The measures we used in this study are type–token ratio (TTR), mean size of paradigms (MSP), information in word structure (WS), word entropy (WH), lemma entropy (LH), inflectional synthesis (IS), and morphological feature entropy (MFH) based on the implementation by Çöltekin and Rama (2022). Section D in Appendix illustrates the details of these measures. We compared our retokenized versions of the Japanese GSD and GSD-LUW treebanks with all the treebanks used in their work. For each treebank, we picked 10 samples of 20,000 tokens and averaged the obtained values over the number of samples. Since Japanese orthography is highly logographic (Sproat and Gutkin, 2021), tokens and lemmas are romanized before computation so that orthographic discrepancies among *hiragana*, *katakana*, and *kanji* are ignored.

5.2 Results

Table 3 summarizes the results for selected treebanks.[7] To compare typological differences, the table demonstrates Japanese treebanks (GSD, GSD-LUW, and their retokenized versions), Vietnamese (analytic), English (weakly analytic), Russian (fusional), and Turkish (agglutinative). For Japanese treebanks, there are overall tendencies where LUW, which treats compound nouns and light verb constructions as one token, is more morphologically complex than SUW. In addition, it is evident that including verbal conjugation and nominal

[7]The codes and full results are published in the forked repository: https://github.com/ctaguchi/mcomplexity.

Language	Typology	Treebank	TTR	MSP	WS	WH	LH	IS	MFH
Japanese	agglutinative	GSD	0.259	1.075	0.318	9.397	9.192	0.0	1.325
		GSD_1	0.263	1.109	0.365	9.600	9.265	9.8	2.583
		GSD_2	0.400	1.471	0.505	11.242	10.241	11.2	3.030
		GSDLUW	0.320	1.082	0.351	9.433	9.223	0.0	1.296
		$GSDLUW_1$	0.338	1.061	0.448	9.600	9.455	9.7	2.619
		$GSDLUW_2$	0.426	1.065	0.464	11.296	11.037	11.6	3.144
Vietnamese	analytic	VTB	0.166	1.0	0.374	9.964	9.966	0.0	1.253
English	weakly analytic	LinES, GUM, ParTUT	0.207	1.210	0.365	9.572	9.176	5.733	3.701
Russian	fusional	SynTagRus, GSD	0.464	1.479	0.489	11.582	10.797	11.5	3.596
Turkish	agglutinative	IMST	0.399	2.277	0.573	11.719	10.0215	13	3.589

Table 3: Comparison of morphological complexities for the original and retokenized treebanks of Japanese and other typologically diverse languages. A subscript 1 indicates our first level of retokenization (verbs) and a subscript 2 indicates our second level (verbs and nouns). For each measure, the greater a value is, the more morphologically complex the language is. Values for languages with multiple treebanks are averaged.

	vi	en	ru	tr
GSD	**0.9998**	0.8631	0.6708	0.5843
GSD_1	0.6720	0.9349	**0.9992**	**0.9907**
GSD_2	0.6691	0.9337	**0.9993**	**0.9932**
GSDLUW	**0.9998**	0.8612	0.6689	0.5823
$GSDLUW_1$	0.6823	0.9390	**0.9988**	**0.9877**
$GSDLUW_2$	0.6713	0.9352	**0.9990**	**0.9890**

Table 4: Pearson correlation matrix for the selected languages and Japanese treebanks. A subscript 1 indicates our first level of retokenization (verbs) and a subscript 2 indicates our second level (verbs and nouns).

case-marking in morphological annotation leads to higher complexity.

We also notice numerical similarities between the conventional Japanese treebanks (GSD and GSDLUW) and the Vietnamese treebank. In fact, Pearson's correlation matrix shown in Table 4 numerically demonstrates that the measured morphological complexities of conventional treebanks are the most similar to Vietnamese, an analytic language. In contrast, the retokenized treebanks have the highest similarity scores with Russian followed by Turkish, which are both synthetic languages. It is notable that Russian and Turkish do not show much contrast despite their typological difference in the degree of fusion. This is likely due to the limitation of the morphological complexity measures used in this experiment which take into account the distribution of tokens, lemmas, and morphological features but do not consider how a token is morphologically derived from a lemma. A possible way to measure fusionality is to measure the edit distance between a lemma and a surface form that is weighted more on substitution and deletion so that agglutinative morphology (insertion) would score lower and be distinguished from fusional inflections.

Regarding IS and MFH, which take into account morphological features in their variables, it is notable that (i) the IS score for the conventional Japanese treebanks is 0 while our retokenized treebanks show much higher complexity (9.7–11.6) rather close to synthetic languages, and (ii) the MFH of our retokenized treebanks stands between an analytic language and synthetic languages. These results reflect the typological characteristics of Japanese as an agglutinative language.

6 Concluding Remarks

This paper has argued for morphology-aware tokenization policies for UD Japanese treebanks and conducted an experiment that measures the morphological complexity of Japanese based on the retokenized treebanks with morphological features. In doing so, we proposed new annotation schemes for tokenization and morphological features in Japanese. The results showed that, although the morphological complexity of the current Japanese UD resembled that of an isolating language, our retokenized treebanks have scores more similar to synthetic languages, which reflect the typological reality of Japanese. The proposed tokenization will also be suitable for developing UD treebanks for other Japanese–Ryukyuan languages that syntactically have a similar structure to Japanese but can be morphologically more fusional. Furthermore, tokenization and morphological annotation conforming to UD's general guidelines enable crosslinguistic comparative studies; therefore, discussions for further cross-treebank consistencies are required.

7 Acknowledgments

I thank Dr. Yugo Murawaki and Dr. So Miyagawa for our discussion about the tokenization policy of current Japanese UD. I am also grateful to Dr. Çağrı Çöltekin for giving us advice on reproducing the results on morphological complexity. This material is based upon work supported by the National Science Foundation under Grant No. BCS-2109709. Any opinions, findings, and conclusions or recommendations expressed in this material are those of the author(s) and do not necessarily reflect the views of the National Science Foundation.

References

Çağrı Çöltekin and Taraka Rama. 2022. What do complexity measures measure? correlating and validating corpus-based measures of morphological complexity. *Linguistics Vanguard*.

Marie-Catherine de Marneffe, Christopher D. Manning, Joakim Nivre, and Daniel Zeman. 2021. Universal Dependencies. *Computational Linguistics*, 47(2):255–308.

Yasuharu Den, Junpei Nakamura, Toshinobu Ogiso, and Hideki Ogura. 2008. A proper approach to Japanese morphological analysis: Dictionary, model, and evaluation. In *Proceedings of the Sixth International Conference on Language Resources and Evaluation (LREC'08)*, Marrakech, Morocco. European Language Resources Association (ELRA).

Martin Haspelmath. 2015. Defining vs. diagnosing linguistic categories: A case study of clitic phenomena. In Joanna Blaszczak, Dorota Klimek-Jankowska, and Krzysztof Migdalski, editors, *How categorical are categories?: New approaches to the old questions of noun, verb, and adjective*, pages 273–304. De Gruyter Mouton, Berlin, München, Boston.

Taku Kudo, Kaoru Yamamoto, and Yuji Matsumoto. 2004. Applying conditional random fields to Japanese morphological analysis. In *Proceedings of the 2004 Conference on Empirical Methods in Natural Language Processing*, pages 230–237, Barcelona, Spain. Association for Computational Linguistics.

Osahito Miyaoka. 2002. 語とはなにか：エスキモー語から日本語をみる (*go to wa nani ka: esukimoogo kara nihongo wo miru*) [*What is a word: looking at Japanese from the perspective of Eskimo*]. Sanseido.

Yugo Murawaki. 2019. On the definition of japanese word.

Graham Neubig, Yosuke Nakata, and Shinsuke Mori. 2011. Pointwise prediction for robust, adaptable Japanese morphological analysis. In *Proceedings of the 49th Annual Meeting of the Association for Computational Linguistics: Human Language Technologies*, pages 529–533, Portland, Oregon, USA. Association for Computational Linguistics.

Joakim Nivre, Marie-Catherine de Marneffe, Filip Ginter, Jan Hajič, Christopher D. Manning, Sampo Pyysalo, Sebastian Schuster, Francis Tyers, and Daniel Zeman. 2020. Universal Dependencies v2: An evergrowing multilingual treebank collection. In *Proceedings of the Twelfth Language Resources and Evaluation Conference*, pages 4034–4043, Marseille, France. European Language Resources Association.

Hideki Ogura, Hanae Koiso, Yumi Fujiike, Sayaka Miyauchi, Hikari Konishi, and Yutaka Hara. 2011. 現代日本語書き言葉均衡コーパス：形態論情報規程集第4版（下） (*Gendai nihongo kakikotoba kinkou koopasu: keitairon zyouhou kiteisyuu dai 4 han (ge)*) [*Balanced Corpus of Contemporary Written Japanese: rules on morphological information Ver. 4 (Vol. 2)*]. 国立国語研究所内部報告書 [Kokuritu kokugo kenkyuuzyo naibu houkokusyo]. National Institute for Japanese Language and Linguistics.

Mai Omura and Masayuki Asahara. 2018. UD-Japanese BCCWJ: Universal Dependencies annotation for the Balanced Corpus of Contemporary Written Japanese. In *Proceedings of the Second Workshop on Universal Dependencies (UDW 2018)*, pages 117–125, Brussels, Belgium. Association for Computational Linguistics.

Gregory Pringle. 2016. Thoughts on the Universal Dependencies proposal for Japanese: The problem of the word as a linguistic unit. `http://www.cjvlang.com/Spicks/udjapanese.html`, Date accessed: November 10, 2022.

Richard Sproat and Alexander Gutkin. 2021. The taxonomy of writing systems: How to measure how logographic a system is. *Computational Linguistics*, 47(3):477–528.

Daniel Zeman et al. 2022. Universal dependencies 2.11. LINDAT/CLARIAH-CZ digital library at the Institute of Formal and Applied Linguistics (ÚFAL), Faculty of Mathematics and Physics, Charles University.

A Glossing Abbreviations

CAU — causative; COP — copula; DAT — dative; IN — inessive; NEG — negative; NMLZ — nominalizer; PASS — passive; PAST — past; POL — polite; PRES — present (non-past); Q — interrogative particle; RESP — respectful form; TOP — topic.

B Verbal and adjectival inflection in Japanese

	Verbs		-*i* adjectives		
Stem form	Ending	*kak-* "to write"	Ending	*naga-* "long"	
Irrealis 未然形	*-a* (*-o*)	*kaka-*, *kako-*	*-karo*	*nagakaro-*	*daro-*
Continuative 連用形	*-i*	*kaki-*, *kai-*	*-ku*, *-kat*	*nagaku-*, *nagakat-*	*de*, *dat-*
Terminal 終止形	*-u*	*kaku*	*-i*	*nagai*	*da*
Attributive 連体形	*-u*	*kaku*	*-i*	*nagai*	*na*
Hypothetical 仮定形	*-e*	*kake-*	*-kere*	*nagakere-*	*nara*
Imperative 命令形	*-e*	*kake*	—	—	—

Table 5: A concise conjugation table for Modern Japanese verbs, -*i* adjectives, and copula.

POS	Form	Feature	Formation	Example
VERB	Negative	`Polarity=Neg`	irr. + *-nai*	*kakanai*
	Passive	`Voice=Pass`	irr. + *-(ra)reru*	*kakareru*
	Causative	`Voice=Cau`	irr. + *-(sa)seru*	*kakaseru*
	Volitional	`Mood=Opt`	irr. + *-(y)ou*	*kakou*
	Polite	`Polite=Form`	cont. + *-masu*	*kakimasu*
	Progressive converb (1)	`Aspect=Prog|VerbForm=Conv`	cont. + *-nagara*	*kakinagara*
	Progressive converb (2)	`Aspect=Prog|VerbForm=Conv`	cont. + *-tutu*	*kakitutu*
	Prospective	`Aspect=Prosp`	cont. + *-sou*	*kakisou*
	Exemplification	`VerbForm=Exem`	cont. + *-tari*	*kaitari*
	Past	`Tense=Past`	cont. + *-ta*	*kaita*
	Past conditional	`Mood=Cnd|Tense=Past`	cont. + *-tara*	*kaitara*
	Converb	`VerbForm=Conv`	cont. + *-te*	*kaite*
	Infinitive	`VerbForm=Inf`	cont. + *-Ø*	*kaki*
	Conditional	`Mood=Cnd`	hyp. + *-ba*	*kakeba*
	Potential	`Mood=Pot`	hyp. + *-ru*	*kakeru*
ADJ	Exemplification	`VerbForm=Exem`	cont. + *-tari*	*nagakattari*
	Past	`Tense=Past`	cont. + *-atta*	*nagakatta*
	Past conditional	`Mood=Cnd|Tense=Past`	cont. + *-attara*	*nagakattara*
	Converb	`VerbForm=Conv`	cont. + *-te*	*nagakute*
	Infinitive	`VerbForm=Inf`	cont. + Ø	*nagaku*
	Conditional	`Mood=Cnd`	hyp. + *-ba*	*nagakereba*

Table 6: Verbal conjugation of Modern Japanese and its correspondence to UD features. Note that `VerbForm=Exem` is a proposed feature that is currently not part of UD features. The abbreviations irr., cont., and hyp. stand for the stem forms (irrealis, continuative, hypothetical, respectively).

C Nominal inflection in Japanese

Case	Feature	Morpheme	*neko* "cat"
Nominative	`Case=Nom`	*-ga*	*neko-ga*
Genitive	`Case=Gen`	*-no*	*neko-no*
Dative	`Case=Dat`	*-ni*	*neko-ni*
Accusative	`Case=Acc`	*-o*	*neko-o*
Lative	`Case=Lat`	*-e*	*neko-e*
Ablative	`Case=Abl`	*-kara*	*neko-kara*
Locative	`Case=Loc`	*-de*	*neko-de*
Comitative	`Case=Com`	*-to*	*neko-to*
Comparative	`Case=Cmp`	*-yori*	*neko-yori*

Table 7: Tentative feature assignment for case particles (*kakuzyosi*; 格助詞).

D Definitions of the measures

The morphological complexity measures by Çöltekin and Rama (2022) are defined as:

$$\text{TTR} := \frac{|\{T\}|}{|T|}$$

$$\text{MSP} := \frac{|\{T\}|}{|\{L\}|}$$

$$\text{WS} := \frac{|T|}{|\text{compress}(T)|} - \frac{|T_{\text{rand}}|}{|\text{compress}(T_{\text{rand}})|}$$

$$\text{WH} := -\sum_i p(t_i) \log p(t_i)$$

$$\text{LH} := -\sum_i p(l_i) \log p(l_i)$$

$$\text{IS} := |\{\Phi\}|$$

$$\text{MFH} := -\sum_i p(\phi_i) \log p(\phi_i),$$

where T is a list of tokens in the sample, $\{\cdot\}$ a set (i.e., without duplication), $|\cdot|$ the length, T_{rand} the sample after randomly changing characters of its tokens, compress$(\cdot)$ a compression function, $p(t_i)$ the probability of a token type t_i, $p(l_i)$ the probability of a lemma type l_i, Φ a list of features used in verbs, and $p(\phi_i)$ the probability of a feature type ϕ_i. In the actual implementation, `zlib`'s compression function was used for measuring WS.

Author Index

Association for Computational Linguistics
209 N. Eighth Street
Stroudsburg, Pennsylvania 18360

ISBN 978-1-7138-9065-2

9 781713 890652

CURRAN ASSOCIATES INC.
proceedings.com

10th Workshop on Natural Language Processing for Computer Assisted Language Learning (NLP4CALL 2021)

Online
31 May 2021